ISRAEL—
A PRECARIOUS SANCTUARY

Studies in Judaism

ISRAEL—
A PRECARIOUS SANCTUARY
War, Death and the Jewish People

By
Eugene and Anita Weiner

UNIVERSITY
PRESS OF
AMERICA

Lanham • New York • London

Copyright © 1989 by

University Press of America®, Inc.

4720 Boston Way
Lanham, MD 20706

3 Henrietta Street
London WC2E 8LU England

Library of Congress Cataloging-in-Publication Data

Weiner, Eugene.
Israel—a precarious sanctuary : war, death, and the
Jewish people / Eugene and Anita Weiner.
p.   cm. — (Studies in Judaism)
Bibliography: p.
Includes index.
1. Israel—History, Military—Psychological aspects.   2. Fear of death.
3. War—Psychological aspects.   4. Mental health—Israel.
I. Weiner, Anita.   II. Title.   III. Series.
DS119.2W44   1989   956.94—dc19   89–5669 CIP

ISBN 0–8191–7441–6 (alk. paper)

Dedication

To Avraham "Patchie" Shapira, from Kibbutz Yizrael. He has selflessly devoted his time, energy, and considerable knowledge to the encouragement of Jewish scholarship in Israel and has ceaselessly encouraged us to publish our thoughts and experiences.

Contents

About the Authors

Eugene Weiner is a graduate of the Jewish Theological Seminary of America's Rabbinical School, and received his doctorate in Sociology from Columbia University. He has taught in the Sociology Department of Haifa University since 1969, and has been Chairman of the Department and Head of Graduate Studies. During the Yom Kippur and Lebanese wars he served as an Officer (reserves) in the Psychological Division of the Israeli army working with combat troops and with bereaved families.

Anita Weiner is a graduate of Barnard College, the Wurzweiler School of Social Work, and received her Doctorate from the Hebrew University of Jerusalem. She has been teaching in the Haifa University School of Social Work since 1969, where she is in charge of Child and Family Studies. She has clinical experience with children and during the Yom Kippur War she worked with many bereaved families through the Israeli Defense Department.

The Weiners live on the Carmel in Haifa, Israel. They have two married sons and four grandchildren living nearby.

Preface

Death is part of all human relations. We understand ourselves by understanding its impact on us and on the society in which we live. Over the past twenty years the authors have attempted to deal with issues of war death and non-violence. What we have written reflects our experience. With our two sons, we, two American Jews, in 1969 began our transition from the America of the 1960s to the Israel of the past eighteen years, from Manhattan to Haifa.

History comprises not only the grand story told by historians. It includes the partial narratives of individuals enmeshed in events of their times, of people attempting to make some emotional and theoretical sense of experience. This book is about history writ small. It makes no claim for scholarly synthesis. We include in it what matters to us about death, war, the Jewish people. The thread running through the issues and events we choose is their centrality to our life in Israel.

Acknowledgements

Although the events of the times were sufficiently dramatic to stimulate our thoughts and emotions, a few individuals focused our ideas and precipitated them into writing. The hour and a half spent with Martin Luther King Jr. was, of course, an unforgettable source of inspiration. Chayim Borochov, administrator in the Psychological Unit of the Army, was exceedingly helpful. "Beno" ran the Haifa Unit of Ktzin HaIr with warmth and efficiency. The wartime experiences in Lebanon were shared daily with Reuven Gal,former Head Officer of the Israel Army Psychological Unit; Chaya Kurtz was the consulting psychologist for work with the terrified child; Kate Schynayerson Ruchana and Carol Gordon were the catalysts for the two letters following the Lebanese war. Finally, we must acknowledge our debt to Robert J. Lifton and the Wellfleet group in the formation of our thinking on the nuclear issues. The framework of our essay is their framework; only its application to the Israeli context is original. Without these people, and many more, our thoughts and experiences would have been impoverished. Our thanks to them all.

We would like to acknowledge with thanks permission to reprint those essays which have been published as articles in various journals. Most of them have been altered, some of them considerably. They appeared as follows: "The Meaning of Munich," *Response*, Vol. VI No. 4, Winter 1972-1973; "Israel's Heroic Dead," *Worldview*, January, 1973, pp. 22-26; "Adult Evaluation of the Young: The Case of Israel's Victorious Youth in the Six-Day War" (tables compiled with Aliza Cohen and Esther Pedorowitz), *The Jewish Journal of Sociology*, Vol. XV: No. 1: June 1973 pp. 107-117; "Letters From the War," *Response*, Vol. VII No. 4, Winter 1973-1974; "The Death Taint and Uncommon Vitality: The Case of the Ever Dying Jewish People," Peretz, D. *Advances in Thanatology*, Vol. 5, No. 2, New York, Arno Press, 1982 pp. 66-78; "The Aborted Sibling Factor: A Case Study," *Clinical Social Work Journal*, Vol. 12, No. 3, Fall 1984, pp. 209-215; both "The Meaning of Munich: Some Thoughts on Germans and Jews," and "Limits and Intentions: A Letter From Israel," *Response*, Winter 1984-1985.

Chapter One

Dying Into Life: the Paradox of Jewish Vitality

We wrote this first essay in the spring of 1974, during the depressing aftermath of the Yom Kippur War. The unanticipated victory of the Six-Day War in 1969 had swept the country with a heady optimism which persisted despite the long War of Attrition that followed. Our piece responds to the universal atmosphere of despair in Israel which now succeeded the euphoria of previous years.

Some existences seem living deaths (Heidegger, 1962; Demske, 1970; Lifton, 1973). And yet, these attenuated lives can be amazingly vital and creative. In this chapter we aim to explore briefly and in broad outline one example of these vital, but attenuated existences, the case of the Jewish People.

The Jewish People's continuance manifests a heroic, unprecedented *tour de force* of religious, cultural and national assertiveness. The State of Israel is its most recent achievement. Nonetheless, the precariousness of existence, which has darkened the reality of Jewish history over the course of centuries, has not been dispelled by the creation of the State (Neusner, 1973). Israel, even with its present existence a certainty, still seems unlikely. This is a strange phenomenon. The desire to establish irrefutably and to normalize Jewish existence figured prominently among forces which brought Israel into being, but the existence of Israel has not dispelled lingering doubts about its reality. Israel continues to bear the stamp of unlikelihood of being and yet not quite being, of life and death – that characterizes all post-exilic Jewish existence.

But is the aspiration for normalization desirable, or does a death-tainted existence have vitality all its own? This question has aroused heated public debate, allowing the death taint to be openly acknowledged – particularly by those who hope to abolish it. One can see in the debate the monumental struggle of a group to make the best of a grim and tragic reality.

And relevance of the debate has been heightened by the particular circumstances in which the State of Israel was established. If ever group life was manifestly vitalized by death, this was the example. In the words of Walter Lacqueur "The war in Europe was over, the world had been liberated from Nazi terror and oppression, peace had returned. For the Jewish people it was the peace of the graveyard. Yet paradoxically at the very time when the 'objective' Jewish question had all but disappeared, the issue of a Jewish State became more topical than ever before... The victors in the war had an uneasy conscience as the stark tragedy of the Jewish People unfolded before their eyes. It was only now that the question was asked whether enough had been done to help them and what could be done for the survivors" (Lacqueur, 1972).

The possibility of using the graveyard as a means towards a more vital existence had been under discussion by the Jewish people long before the Second World War. Indeed, one can find traces of such a thrust in the thought and action of the Jewish people from its earliest historical records. It was a perspective conditioned by historical circumstances and by mythic paradigms that sought to tap the vitalizing power of death.

One of the more salient images over the years has been that of the *living dead*. The relatively emancipated Jews of the Eighteenth and Nineteenth centuries focused on this image as a negative indication of their unlikely existence. In their condemnatory and critical attitude towards the image they bear eloquent, albeit reluctant witness to the powerful grip it held over their consciousness. Indeed, they saw in this uncanny and ambiguous condition the starting point for those revitalization movements they were partial to.

As Pinsker, an early spokesman for the new Jewish national rebirth, wrote in 1882, "Thus the world saw in this people (the Jews) the frightening form of the dead walking among the living. This ghostlike apparition of a people without unity or organization, without land or other bond of union, no longer alive, and yet moving among the living – This eerie form scarcely paralleled in history, unlike anything that preceded or followed it, could not fail to make a strange and peculiar impression upon the imagination of nations. And if the fear of ghosts is something inborn, and has a certain justification in the psychic life of humanity, is it any wonder that it asserted itself powerfully at the sight of this dead yet living nation? Fear of the Jewish ghost has been handed down and strengthened for generations and centuries. It led to a prejudice which, in its turn, in connection with other forces... paved the way for Judeophobia" (Pinsker, 1966).

Pinsker developed a theory of anti-semitism based on the notion that "for the living, the Jew is a dead man," The way to deal with this moribund condition was to "devote all of our remaining moral force to reestablish ourselves as a living nation so that we may finally assume a more fitting and dignified role" (Pinsker, 1966). Pinsker, like many of the proto-nationalist figures of the late Nineteenth century, acknowledged the aptness of the living dead image for the Jew and desired to transcend it.

In their zeal to infuse a less eccentric and, in their eyes, a more bountiful life force into the Jewish people, these early nationalists gave short shrift to the death taint, an image which has proven to have a rather extraordinary life force of its own. If there is one constant characteristic that has accompanied the Jewish people over its four thousand year history, it is that of being perceived as moribund, and as the subject of a premature obituary. The British Museum possesses a monument from the Thirteenth century before the Common Era on which is written "Israel is desolated, its seed is no more." Some desolation, some seed! Indeed, if the living dead survive with such extraordinary longevity, then the status must surely be worthy of analysis, particularly for those seeking to understand group survival.

Within the image of the living dead Jews there are two paradoxical, and, at times, contradictory themes. First, the Jews are tainted with death because they have lived too long, and second, Jews are tainted with death because they lack an indispensably vital part of life. According to the first theme, the Jews are a freakish anomaly of endurance, and according to the second, they are a compositional monstrosity lacking a necessary precondition for life. Both functional and structural defects are implied, but the contradictions between them have not been noted. If life is defined as the possession of certain vital traits, and these traits do not exist, then how is it possible to live at all, and then to live such a protracted life? These mutually contradictory implications did not prevent the two notions from reinforcing and supplementing each other in practice. The Jews are seen as the living dead because they have lived too long and also because they have a mortal defect and are thus not fully alive.

These dual primary themes appear to have been reinforced by two further attitudes held by Christian theologians and often elaborated by Jews. First, the Jews were stigmatized because not only did they not acknowledge the proffered savior of the world, worse than that, they allegedly crucified him. To be responsible for the death of a God is to provoke forces threatening to one's existence. In a sense, killing God is murdering life. The mortal punishment may be temporarily postponed, but its advent is a certainty. Second, the Jews were witness to the recurring murderous attempts of others to annihilate them. They were mistreated victims whose continuing existence reminded those capable of empathy that they remained the potential targets of murderous intent. The image of the living dead Jew, murdered in the past and potential murder victims of the future, colored the perception of even sympathetic outsiders.

The notion of the living dead became a social stigma with great force and power. All living beings are marked for ultimate death, but the death taint stigma as applied to the Jewish people is different. It singles them out and marks them for an immoderate, indelible, particularly unseemly fate. The Jewish people are seen as the living who are more dead than alive. They are symbolically dead by virtue of having *sentenced identities*. As individuals, they are like convicted murderers who have been sentenced to death and await execution, or sufferers of fatal diseases who have been diagnosed and pronounced incurable. As a group, they are like uprooted, displaced tribes of natives, phased out organizations or conquered nationalities assigned for extirpation, decimation or annihilation.

In the case of the individual, the death taint is a matter of the relationship between the self and the body, which is an "injured one." "The self remains shackled to a body seen as somehow already dead, or permanently injured in some inexplicable way" (Lifton, 1973). It is "a relationship seen as fundamentally incompatible with life, between two independent, indispensable parts of existence," one of which is irrevocably defective" (Caswell, 1972).

If the sentence is annulled or found to have been inappropriately pronounced, on rare occasions a sentenced identity can be transformed into a *reprieved identity*. In such infrequent cases, the injury is somehow repaired and the defective part of the existence is remedied. But most sentences are executed and most sentenced identities expire. The bearers of these identities suffer the taint of their ultimate (future yet present) mortal end.

In addition to the sentenced and the reprieved identities, there is the sentenced identity which is never executed. These are the *sentence-deferred identities*. The taint of death is on them, but execution is continuously and unaccountably deferred. The possessors of these identities exist in a kind of dubiously protected limbo. Theirs is the remarkable but unenviable power of life. Such is the case of the Jewish people, at least as viewed by others, and on occasion, by Jews themselves (Yehoshua, 1972).

In this third identity, the death taint is indelible. A renewed or more natural form of life, which could disprove the existence of the taint, is thus regarded as unnatural. Throughout much of the collective history of the Jewish people any action consequently was regarded as obscene. Action offended modesty and decency; it overstepped some limit of propriety. To take action, for a Jew, would be like one of Lifton's *Hibakuscha*, a Hiroshima victim ("The explosion-affected person, those who permanently encounter death") transferring his defect genetically to his death-tainted progeny, who could never die out. Who would be interested in discovering the secret of their group longevity or in emulating their lives? Their longevity would be regarded as a somewhat obscene, protracted doom, rather than a meritorious achievement.

The Jews are rarely given credit for heroic endurance. Considering the fascination that longevity generally elicits, this is strange. If there indeed had been someone called Methusalah, and he actually had lived 969 years, he no doubt would have spent most of his time answering questions about how he had managed to live so long. Most cultures have a concept of what constitutes a reasonable life span, and those who exceed these limits are usually the object of intense interest. Expeditions of physicians and physical anthropologists have made their way to Andean villages, Pakistani settlements or Caucasian farms in order to locate and examine the extraordinarily long-lived. The interest evinced is usually not only scientifically motivated, but appears to have a quality of awe. It is as if an uncommon endurance marked with continued vitality is intrinsically heroic. The very existence of such dynamic longevity is an encouraging testament to the battle against decay, decomposition and death.

The Jewish people, however, do not receive such adulation. Longevity apparently evokes not only awe. People who spectacularly surpass a reasonable life expectancy are not only venerable. They can be, and frequently are, ridiculous. Uncommon old age can be viewed not just as incredible, but also as incredible absurdity, a bit preposterous. Time has been borrowed from death's domain for an unnaturally prolonged duration. What should be defunct is freakishly alive; what should be deceased is vigorous. Thus an unnatural endurance can itself become an indication of the death taint. Keeping death at bay can be considered improper. Endurance is not automatically associated with moral grandeur if such endurance is tainted with death.

It is the predisposition to value a particular kind of prolonged life which resolves the ambivalence towards uncommon longevity. In the case of the abnormally long-lived Jewish people there is frequently no such positive predisposition. The Jewish people are rarely given credit for existing remarkably long compared to most nations, religions and civilizations (Elazar, 1969). Great civilizations rarely continue to exist longer than a millennium, and most last a good deal less. The Jewish people has an unbroken connection with its own cultural past for four millennia.

This connection is relatively unadulterated by extrinsic foreign influences. Whether the cultural forms developed be in the area of language, values, norms, customs, literature or myth, those of the ancient past are substantially the same and are recognizable in the forms of today. Where are the paeans of praise for this heroic achievement of endurance? Who is trying to emulate the Jewish experience? In the eyes of many, on the contrary, this ability to endure is a questionable virtue.

Another alleged requisite for national life and survival which the Jewish people has existed without for much of its history is a land. Their own land. By not having their own land during much of Jewish history the Jewish people became archetypal wanderers whose dismal journeys and imperiled settlements forever emphasized their vulnerability (Roshwald, 1972). It is this very vulnerability which emphasizes their talents for survival. How could a nation so lacking the ecological prerequisites for life be so long-lived? How could this people refuse to buckle and crumble despite a congenital structural morbidity?

Losing its land two millennia ago did not cause the Jewish people to die a normal death. Its continuance arose from the abnormal circumstances surrounding its birth. From its inception, the Jewish people had an unusual relationship to its land. The attachment was not simply based on geographical proximity, on being born and raised on the land. The connection was a special one.

In the Biblical account of the corporate birth of the Jewish people, be it the covenant of Abraham or the revelation at Sinai, the context of the birth is alien, the promise is home. In other words, home is not a taken-for-granted reality where being *starts*, but rather, according to mythic account, a promised goal to be attained, a place where being may be *enhanced*. Attaining the title to the promised land is perpetually achieved and constantly legitimated. It is achieved through obstinate striving and legitimated through virtuous action. It is a project to *enhance* an imperfect existence rather than a *given* of reality. Home is not where you come from, but rather where you are going – even if you are there already. The promised land is an intrinsically unfulfillable promise, if we consider fulfillment a once-and-for-all time matter.

Even when the Jews were living in the land, the promised goal remained relevant. Their hold on the land was always tenuous, partially because of the powerful enemies who were ever seeking to dislodge them from it. So there was never a period when Jewish settlement in the land could be taken for granted. And when not radically threatened by enemies from without, the land was threatened from within. Consequently, there was hardly a period in Jewish history when a leader could justifiably claim that the promise of the land was unambiguously fulfilled. For this reason, the Jewish people can accurately be described as a group of perpetual homecomers.

At its inception the Jewish religion was already a "religion on wheels," as characterized by Isaiah Berlin. One of the first corporate acts of group commitment was a willingness to travel *towards* the land. This movement does not stop even with death. One of the eschatological visions of the "final days" has the bones of the scattered Jewish dead rolling under the ground towards the promised land. They are homecomers all. Even Jewish bones not already brought to the promised land are mobile bones according to the mythic vision. Thus, from the beginning Jews have had a double relationship to the land. The group was able to cohere without the land, but their most deeply sacred vocation was defined as a striving to achieve that land. Once achieved, however tenuously, the land and the people must constantly be perfected and enhanced or the results would be dire.

What dire result? – Death.

To the Jew it has always appeared safer to die in the promised land, or to be buried there, than to live there. The grim and not unlikely possibility always exists that one will be consumed in life by the very promised land which is supposed to supplement an imperfect existence. Not only was the land a desirable but illusive quest, it was also an inherently dangerous one; it was hard to say whether the Jew was safer with or without it. Actual settlement of the land could take place only if conduct was proper. Above all else, the land was a holy land, filled with both benevolent and malevolent powers. These powers could be activated by behavior not in accord with the revealed divine will.

And the land did not belong to the Jewish people alone. It was held in trust by them, but that trust was dependent upon God's promise. As long as the Jewish people were God's, the land was theirs. They had their part of the bargain to keep. So long as they were faithful to their mission their connection with the land could persist. Should they be unfaithful, the land would spew them forth and they would be purged from it amidst death and plunder. Like themselves, the land was set aside for a purpose. It was to be the scene for great and extraordinary happenings. This too was the meaning of a holy land. Should the Jewish people fulfill their divinely appointed purpose, the land would be the scene of their elevation and apotheosis. Should they betray that purpose then the land would consume them.

One finds in the Biblical narratives a constant connection between the land and death (Brichto, 1973). While the land was infinitely desirable, it was also mortally dangerous. It was Abraham's desire to bury Sarah that led to the first purchased title to the land. However, the desire for a resting place was confronted continually by the prophetic warning that improper conduct would lead to undignified death of large numbers of people, and to the expulsion of the remainder from the land.

There were times when the death warnings and threats of expulsion were realized. The destruction of a large portion of the people by the Assyrians in 722 B.C.E., and the decimation of the population and the expulsion by the Babylonians in 586 B.C.E., gave much added credence to the prophetic threat. With the early memories of exile in Egypt, there was much communal history to strengthen the belief in the prophetic threat of a break between the land and the people. All these cultural memories served as forewarnings of the great exile yet to come.

When the great dispersion started in 70 C.E. Jewish consciousness had embedded in it memories of mass killings and exiles which ended, for the most part, with the resettlement of the land. These previous exiles had provided the people with an opportunity to deal with exile and mass death as a *conceivable* part of national life. Almost from its inception, the group prepared itself for a most deprived existence. These historical precedents and the particular structure of group consciousness which developed in response enabled the Jews to exist for two millennia without a land. The ability to compensate for the loss of the land, and not to be demoralized, can certainly be regarded as an extraordinary instance of collective elan.

The Jewish people have been throughout their history extraordinarily creative and alive, despite their anomalous death taint and the corresponding functional and structural defects. Everything written thus far hardly prepares one for an appreciation of these achievements. How is it that a people so dead can be so alive? Living on borrowed time without the necessary means for proper group life has not proven to be a hindrance at all.

Rawidowicz, in a brilliant, polemical and largely ignored essay has argued, convincingly I believe, that it was precisely the imminence of collective death that activated and energized the latent creative collective impulses.

> Yet making all allowances for the general motives in this dread of the end, it has nowhere been at home so incessantly, with such acuteness and intensity as in the House of Israel. The world may be constantly dying but no... nation was ever so incessantly dying... as Israel... I am

often tempted to think that this fear of cessation in Israel was fundamentally a kind of protective individual and collective emotion. Israel has indulged so much in the fear of its end that its constant vision of the end helped it to overcome every crisis, to emerge from every threatened end as a living unit, though much wounded and reduced. In anticipating the end it became its master. Thus no catastrophe would ever take this end-fearing people by surprise so as to knock it off its balance, still less to obliterate it – as if Israel's incessant preparation for the end made this end absolutely impossible... As far as historical reality is concerned we are confronted here with a phenomenon which has almost no parallel in mankind's story: a nation that has been disappearing constantly for the last 2,000 years exterminated in dozens of lands, all over the globe, reduced to half or third of its population by tyrants ancient and modern, and yet, re-equips itself for a new start, a second and third chance, always fearing the end, never afraid to make a new beginning, to snatch triumph from the jaws of defeat, whenever and wherever possible. There is no nation more dying than Israel, yet none better equipped to resist disaster (Rawidowicz, 1966).

In contrast to Pinsker's view of the Jewish people, tainted with death, pleading for a normal existence, we find in Rawidowicz a different emphasis. It is not that death has invaded Jewish existence, or that Jews are constituted by a peculiar morbidity. What is characteristic of the group, on the contrary, is its extraordinary *fear* of death. This is an inordinate fear which leads to anticipatory preventive measures so that the end does not come. It is the fear and the anticipatory measures which are triggered, which are the real defense against disaster.

What is stressed in Rawidowicz's analysis, and ignored in Pinsker's, is the appropriateness of preparation for the death-dealing onslaught. To Pinsker, what is important is *discarding the tainted status*. The primary need is for a normal, more whole and complete existence. A living death can only be remedied by a full life. For Rawidowicz, a full life devoid of the inordinate death fear is the greatest peril for continued survival. If the group death has been defeated time and again by anticipations, however morose (but nonetheless based on proven realities), who is to say what would happen to the group without such anticipations? The Jewish people have cried "Wolf, wolf" tirelessly, believing the cry almost every time, making necessary precautions, and then have had the experience of the wolf arriving with devastating frequency.

Rawidowicz believes in the positive value of 1) the warning; 2) the collective belief in the warning; 3) the taking of precautions against the threat; 4) the assumption of continuously threatening realities. For him, living as an "ever dying people" is the surest guarantee for survival. The ultimate threat is security and quietude. Not so for

Pinsker. For him, the contamination of the death taint prevents a proper existence. It is a kind of curse, a fate to be deplored and if possible remedied *completely*. It is the aspiration for a new life, not the fear of death, which is to be the primary motive force.

What we have revealed in these two attitudes is not simply an incidental polemic on the way in which reality was grasped by the Jewish people. We see in them the modern manifestation of a basic, centuries old, dichotomous response of the culture to its difficult situation. Of the two approaches it is the second, that portrayed by Rawidowicz, which appears to us the more dominant response of the Jewish people to its reality. The aspiration for a new birth, as represented in the first approach, was also preserved in messianic aspirations and embedded in the corporate imagination. To live a half-life, yes, while refusing to give up the dream of a full one. It was the aspiration for the full life which made the half-life bearable, but it was the ability to lead the half-life that made the cultural and historical continuity possible.

In order for a culture to survive and flourish in morbid conditions, it may have to develop anticipatory attitudes and institutions. This is evidently difficult for a culture to do, as Nelson has indicated:

> Civilizations do not end with a bang or a whimper. Civilizations generally die laughing. The more closely great societies approach the point of checkmate, the deeper the indulgence of great numbers in their favorite games. In fact, the worse the situation the more hectic the abandonment. It is when all is fun and joy, on the go-go when the dancers in the charades are on the edge of ecstasy and frenzy, that the hoped for oblivion prevails. At this juncture, treasured elements of the legacy of civilizations slip unnoticed out of focus (Nelson, 1973)

While Nelson's description may be apt for most civilizations, it is not true for the Jews. It was precisely their ability to anticipate the "point of checkmate" and allow for another move – just one more – and another and another, that characterized them more completely. It was the refusal to allow a forgetful and reality-denying ecstasy that was the most typical of Jewish responses to disaster. Life itself was viewed as a context of real and potential disaster, and the main task was to prepare for it.

Preparing for disaster means many things and we will attempt to enumerate only a few. It requires a pervasive philosophy of trust that God will never let the end come within historical time. It further means not making one's survival depend on things that can be taken away. Thus the people currently develop a theodicy of defeat that justifies any misfortune and build their basic institutions so that dispersal will not compromise them. They preserve the maximum of autonomy over their communal affairs through an all-inclusive social welfare system covering all needs and occasions, and cultivate symbolic escape valves to express aggression against their oppressors and thereby to prevent premature, adventitious and self-defeating uprisings. As part of their preparation for disaster, the Jewish people necessarily prolong the crisis mentality, enacting at regular intervals an elaborate social drama and religious ritual with the theme of ultimate return to the land. This in turn requires near universal literacy if these lessons are to be rehearsed by the individual in his own private study. Patterned behavior is equally important. The group has to regulate as much as possible of the intimate life of members and to develop a repertoire of strategies for the handling of various kinds of disasters. Preparation for disaster also means assiduously protecting boundaries of membership so that no matter how dispersed, the group's membership always is clearly defined. As a function of group coherence daily and weekly gatherings of members lend the group a reality for all to see and feel. Imminent disaster further necessitates regarding oneself as superior to one's oppressors (no matter how powerful or intellectually impressive they are). Endurance and continuity are to be regarded as the real test of culture, not power and influence. Remembering one's past glory and making the memory contemporarily relevant, believing in the group's ultimate vindication, being devoted to continuity of the tradition while having social mechanisms to interpret and decide extraordinary events also figure largely. Finally, the group must have protectors whose self esteem and self interest is served and enhanced by the existence of its half-life, and appeal to the conscience even of those who have killed its members to help it continue living. These are only a few of the means that the Jewish people used to preserve its remarkably fragile existence.

Evidently, the question for the Jewish people was never "to be or not to be," but rather how to be while not quite being. And it was the preparation for, accommodation to, and temporary acceptance of that state of not quite being that contributed to the group's extraordinary longevity.

The question that has concerned us in this chapter is how a culture relates to the possibility of its own demise. This is a question that has concerned the Jewish people from its first formative moments of collective being. We have indicated that this concern has contributed to the group's prolonged existence. In the story of the sacrifice of Isaac, Abraham, his father and the promised progenitor of a people, is assured a fruitful posterity and at the same instant commanded to destroy the agent of its realization, his son Isaac. His willingness to endanger his only son, and to live an endangered half-life in which he has only his failing flesh to rely on proves his worthiness.

We have purposely not dealt with the Jewish beliefs of immortality, resurrection, martyrdom or other death-related theories. These beliefs are well documented, and are related to questions not specifically raised in this chapter. We have also not attempted to deal with the complex social and religious factors and circumstances which structured the varying responses to the concept of the ever dying people. What we have tried to do is to make plausible the thesis that the extraordinary longevity of the Jewish people has been dependent upon and intimately connected with their willingness to live a diminished existence.

Chapter Two

Warring for Identity

Today, transformations of identity in the Jewish world still can be as dramatic as those of the early pioneers to pre-state Israel. The image of the small town eastern European merchant transformed into a muscular farmer in the Galillee has become a familiar part of Zionist history. The transformations of today are only less recorded and less synthesized.

Autobiography and biography can help us to understand larger social forces. They can provide a key to the transformations of identity which take place in individuals who move from one life context to another. Those experiences recorded in this chapter occurred from 1965-1988. They are a chronicle of personal thoughts and experiences.

The intense civil rights struggle in 1965, in Selma, Alabama, provides the context for "Non-Violence: A Lasting Transformation?" "Variations on the Need to Resist" comprises four attempts to accommodate in this context the need to resist. First, we take Israel's euphoria after the Six-Day War and its slump into shock through the trauma of the Munich Massacre. Then we explore in turn the meaning and ramification of the Yom Kippur and Lebanon Wars, going back a second time to delve more deeply into the dilemmas posed by Lebanon. The chapter closes with two recent cases of "passive" resistance, one Israeli, one Palestinian, both problematic.

A. Non-Violence: A Lasting Transformation?

Written January, 1972

Some events in life stand out as potent symbols of the past, encompassing important parts of experience. Such an event, for me, was my meeting with Martin Luther King Jr.

The thing that got me angry that March day in 1964 (five years before I moved to Israel with my family), was my sense of remoteness from an important moral struggle. I was serving as a Conservative Rabbi in the Canadian town of Hamilton, Ontario, while in Selma,

Alabama the police had set dogs on human beings and had clubbed defenseless people who were marching for the right to register and to vote. Perhaps the very contrast between the comfortable existence of a middle class Jew whose moral struggles lacked heroic proportions and the patent justice of the Black cause made me ripe for action. The moral struggles of the Jew for greater security in north America lacked an important element towards the mobilization of emotional response. They lacked a believable enemy.

I called a friend who had connections in the Civil Rights Movement, and he gave me the name of a friend of Martin Luther King living in Selma, a Mrs. Selma Jackson. On the phone I asked her this simple question: could a Rabbi from Canada help in the struggle taking place in Selma. She answered yes. Only the day before a Protestant Minister, James Reeb, had been clubbed to death while coming out of a restaurant in Selma. Now a call went out to clergy everywhere to "come to Selma." I had received my invitation.

The invitation was, of course, not only a personal one, so I called some of the Christian clergymen with whom I worked on various ecumenical issues. I called an Anglican Priest, a United Church Minister, a Baptist Minister. In no time flat I found six Ministers who were willing to go to Selma with me and we were on our way. While on the plane I had time to ask myself again and again why I was going, since I knew very well there would be physical danger awaiting us in Alabama. The answer was always the same. It was the moral authority of the man, of Martin Luther King.

Dr. King had assumed the leadership of the civil rights struggle ten years before. He had organized a successful boycott of the Montgomery, Alabama bus system after Mrs. Rosa Parks had refused to give up her seat to a white man in December, 1955. For me, King had one quality which I admired above all else; he had authenticity. His gifts as orator, organizer and writer were of little importance to me. What mattered was that he was a real person connected with a just cause and that he was unafraid to face the consequences of his convictions. Those consequences had included imprisonment and the bombing of his home.

Looking back at this time in my life, I question why, as a Jew in the Diaspora, I became involved in fighting for the interests of a group other than my own. Was there not enough of a moral cause in insuring the survival and well-being of the State of Israel? At the very moment I was agonizing about going to Selma, kibbutz members from Ashdot Yaakow and Moaz Chaim were entering fields that had been mined during the night. Their struggle was constant. Why was it not mine? It seems to me that the answer to this question lies in the remainder of this essay, in the ongoing events and my inner responses to the next few days in Selma.

When the plane landed in Montgomery, we were met by a man who said he was there to bring to Selma those who had responded to the summons. He took us on the road where a few days earlier a northern woman volunteer had been brutally shot and killed. The two things I remember about that ride were the helicopter flying overhead throughout, and the masses of dead moss hanging from the trees. In Canada there was still clean white snow on the ground, and here in Alabama there was dead moss on the trees. It seemed ominous.

We were brought to a Catholic hospital where we would be staying. But immediately we set out again for Brown's Chapel, where a confrontation was taking place between the Civil Rights activists and local law enforcers. My big decision as I walked was whether or not to wear a Kippa (a traditional head covering). Generally I wore my Kippa only for religious services, but here in Selma I wanted to be identified as a Jew. Without such identification, the symbolic importance of my presence would be lessened. I put it on my head, and as I walked to the Chapel I was amazed to be greeted by Black families sitting on the porches of their broken down shacks. "Welcome to Selma, Rabbi" was what I heard from all sides. I was needed here. I was doing something important. I was doing it instead of only talking about it.

As participants in a non-violent struggle, the first thing we had to learn was nonviolence, i.e. how to respond to violence without resorting to violence ourselves. As we walked into the Church a simulation of a police beating was taking place. There were priests, ministers and nuns lying on the floor while standing above them five or six people waved rolled up newspapers in their hands. They were "beating" the participants and saying to them "guard your head and your sexual organs" for that is where the police hit first. As I watched them I was grateful that I had two hands to protect the two sensitive areas at the same time. On the side of the room I heard a group of young blacks say to one another "this is a lot of shit; just let those cops try beating me, I'll show them. This non-violent stuff is for the birds."

Just a few steps from the Chapel was the confrontation line. On one side of a barrier in the street stood a few hundred blacks and clergy singing freedom songs, and on the other side were State Troopers with heavy clubs in their hands and helmets on their heads. Their facial expressions were as coarse and unfeeling as I had imagined. They were all taller than I and about forty kilo heavier, and they certainly were not there for a pleasure outing. At a moment's notice, it seemed, they might start their clubs swinging.

We all took turns manning the line in the street. The watch went on this way day and night for two days. Everyone felt that something big was going to happen.

Inside Brown's Chapel, people were singing continuously for hours. They all spoke about the impending confrontation with Sheriff Jim Clark: there was a great air of expectancy. Martin Luther King was going to lead the procession from Selma to Montgomery, the State capital, to demand the right to register to vote. Rumors were rife about his coming.

Some beautiful people inhabited Brown's Chapel. There was a nun from the Midwest, wearing the white habit of a nursing order. Almost six feet tall, all in white, young, beautiful, she stood in the pulpit talking about things that religious people are supposed to talk about – love, peace, forgiveness, sacrifice, oneness, devotion, and above all non-violence. Yes, yes, yes. It was all clear to me at that moment. Even if it meant having to die. This was all worth dying for.

The nun in white was joined by an array of figures that I have not seen since. The Archbishop of the Greek Orthodox church, the head of the Baptist Churches of Atlanta, an albino black man who sang some haunting spirituals. The church seemed filled with charismatic figures. The air was luminescent with the rightness of it all. Eating was an act of sacrilege during these ethereal moments, and sleeping was out of the question. We were all preparing ourselves for the great moment in much the same way that the Children of Israel prepared themselves for the moment at Sinai.

I met Mrs. Selma Jackson by accident. Someone asked "Mrs. Jackson, where are the rolls?" Mrs. Jackson!... "Are you Mrs. Selma Jackson?" She invited me to her home the next morning to meet with Martin Luther King and Ralph Abernathy, who were staying there. King had been an old boyfriend of hers. She and her husband, who was a dentist in the Black community, were hosting King and Abernathy during their time in Selma.

Getting into the Jackson home was not easy. There were policemen everywhere, and hundreds of media people. Once inside, however, it was quiet and dark. Everything in the home was old, worn and loved. The home seemed the counterpart to Brown's Chapel. I expected the door to open and a rainbow light to bathe us all in multiple colors. But something different, though just as wonderful, was about to happen.

Ralph Abernathy walked into the living room with a towel wrapped around him, and dripping from a shower he had just taken. Shortly after, King walked in similarly attired. They both sat in the living room as they were, talking to me about the day ahead. They were planning to defy the ordinance against marching, and to lead a demonstration to the Selma Court House. Anything could happen.

I really do not remember the details of our conversation that morning. I was too tired and overcome by the intensity of the experience. We discussed Jews, non-violence, Israel, the struggle ahead, the northern Black. It was the emotional climate of the meeting which was important to me more than the content. A moment of confrontation was approaching when everything in us was going to be tested.

What impressed me about King, Abernathy, and Andrew Young, who joined us later, was their calm, determination and professionalism. King seemed eager to respond to challenging questions. He sought the kind of questions that would force him to consider ever more deeply why he chose his present course of action. He seemed to be saying to us "Ask me more penetrating questions that go beneath the superficial trappings of my movement and actions, for it is only through such challenge that I can know the meaning of my behavior." For ten years he had been struggling and his identity had taken shape around responses to challenges. The two overwhelming aspects of his personality were his gentleness and his thoughtfulness. The impression one had while talking to him was that he was willing to consider any thought seriously, and that there was no one he would not treat with kindness.

I found the contrasts in our situation awe-inspiring. Outside, the White people of Selma were boiling with hatred at the intrusion of so many who had come to challenge their way of life. There was a wild commotion on the streets. And there were thousands at Brown's Chapel praying, singing, discussing, planning. News media from around the world were waiting for what would happen next. But here was King wrapped in a towel, in the living room of a former girlfriend, evidently enjoying a good conversation.

The mood in that living room was one of contemplation. In spite of all his personal magnetism, King managed to convince those around him that it was his movement, not himself, which had charisma. As an individual he was accessible, and ready to meet on a level of equality. He seemed eager to break through the mystic aura surrounding those who have been elevated to larger than human dimensions by mass adulation. This need of his for engagement seemed a genuine one, not simply a technique to gain more disciples. He also had a profound respect for Jews, with which I was much impressed. From the beginning, his movement had been helped by Jews. King not only acknowledged this help, but showed a deep commitment to and responsibility for the well-being of the Jewish people.

An hour and a quarter after the start of our conversation, King went to dress for the coming confrontation. That afternoon, the same King walked into Brown's Chapel. But the conditions were not the same. Those who heard him in Brown's Chapel will not forget what he said. The words he spoke that afternoon he repeated in Montgomery, at the end of the march:

> Today I want to tell the city of Selma. Today I want to say to the people of America and the nations of the world: We are not about to turn around. We are on the move now. Yes, we are on the move and no wave of racism can stop us.
>
> We are on the move now. The burning of our churches will not deter us. We are on the move now. The bombing of our homes will not dissuade us. We are on the move now. The beating and killing of our clergymen and young people will not divert us. We are on the move now. The arrest and release of known murderers will not discourage us. We are on the move now... Let us therefore continue our triumph and march... Let us march on segregated housing... Let us march on segregated schools... Let us march on poverty... Let us march on ballot boxes... My people, my people, listen! The battle is in our hands...

These were the words that moved us that day. Martin Luther King was the leader of all good men. In those days it seemed clear that our march would lead to something.

The marches of those years did lead to some improvement in the situation of the Black community in America. There has been some progress in Black housing, schooling, and political power in the United States, but not nearly enough to satisfy those Blacks who were in the cellar of Brown's Chapel and who said "shit." The inheritors of King are anything but non-violent. The philosophical, long-suffering and religious mood of the southern Black has given way to the angry, frustrated, faceless and explosive fury of the northern ghetto Black who is not going to kneel down for any White man. And the respect and mutuality between Black and Jew has turned into self-conscious defensiveness and recrimination.

What have those marches led to for the Jews who participated? In Birmingham Alabama, Albany Georgia, Washington D.C., Chicago Illinois there were thousands and thousands of Jews who were moved much the same way that I was in Brown's Chapel, Selma Alabama. Where are these Jews now?

A great disenchantment has set in among American Jews; they are lying low these days. The American Jewish community has all but repudiated its part in the civil rights struggle. And instead of receiving uncritical gratitude from the Black community for active participation, the Jewish community has been attacked. The northern urban Black sees the Jew as an exploiting White man, and is not grateful for past help. He feels that the Jews who participated with King were not really part of the Black civil rights movement anyway.

Those of us Jews who marched with King in the mid-sixties found ourselves in a peculiar situation during the 1967 war in Israel. Identification with Israel put us in a strange bind. Participation in the non-violent movement of the American Blacks had sapped our will to resist with violence when non-violence as a technique would not work. The experience of exposing one's body to the blows of a southern Sheriff and his henchmen had worked its way into our consciousness. My feeling was that if I was willing to put myself in danger for a moral principle, if I still insisted on a non-violent reaction to evil, why shouldn't everyone, everywhere... including Jews. During those same years, in the late 1960's, the abhorrence of violence as a solution to problems was further reinforced by the traumas of the Vietnam war.

For the first time in my life, I was able to understand how large masses of people could passively accept when violence was inflicted on them. In order to react violently to an aggressor one must not only anticipate his aggression, but prepare oneself psychologically to react with counter violence. Just as training is needed in non-violent techniques before one can become a pacifist, so training is needed in order to react with violence.

In 1967, when the State of Israel faced war and danger, the American Jews marched down Riverside Drive in New York City just as some of us had marched in Selma for the Black civil rights struggle. King's dream of non-violence haunted us. What was missing for some was the relevance of his dream to the situation of Israel. Being an American Jew was not the same as being a southern Black.

Two years later I came on aliya to Israel with my family. As I went through my army training in the early 1970's I found myself having to confront experiences from Brown's Chapel. Here I was learning to shoot an Uzi and throw a hand grenade; there I learned how to take a beating and not react violently. Here I was learning to shoot; there I was learning to love. Here I was being trained to be a soldier; there I had learned a different kind of soldiering.

Martin Luther King was killed by an act of violence. As King's own death demonstrates, pacifism does not work in all situations. Nonetheless, those of us who had the privilege of being a part of his dream still love the memory of him. My meeting with him in 1964 deeply impressed me, and much of my transformation of identity since I came to Israel has been a response to my memories of Selma, and of King's non-violent dreams.

Epilogue

The need to resist violence with violence when passive resistance is doomed to failure creates the conditions for endless brutalization. But what is the alternative? In the Middle East there is little hope for effective passive resistance without a corresponding commitment to martyrdom – and we Jews have had enough of living as a martyred people.

Evidently violence cannot offer a permanent means of resolving conflicts. If it becomes permanent, then the forces of darkness finally have won. Times change, people change, and situations are fluid – obvious truths. Behavior must be reactive both to realistic constraints and to possibilities for change if it is to be moral.

Both passive resistance and violence ultimately fail as solutions to the dilemmas of survival. The only acceptable moral alternative is a direct confrontation between the desire to live, a sense of moral decency, and the courage to confront enemies set on one's destruction. As in any direct communication, personal transformations can then take place.

We have experienced clear-cut provocations which require a reassessment of non-violence. The terrorist attacks in Munich, and the surprise armed invasion during the Yom Kippur War were such provocations. Much less clear is the case of the pre-emptive invasion in the Lebanese War. The moral certainty with which the two letters about Lebanon in this section were written seem retrospectively based on an unreflective and unquestioning certainty. Although we are not apologetic about the role we played in the conflict, we regret the fact that we missed the moral ambiguities of the conflict in our initial responses which are here included.

In retrospect it would appear that Kate and Carol were closer to the moral core of the conflict than we were. The problematic intentions of some of the Israeli military leaders helped to poison the climate and made dying in this war more questionable. A few short weeks after writing letters we thus found ourselves in the Tel Aviv City Hall Square protesting a War which we had justified to our friends weeks before in letters and conversation. Proving once more, if we needed any proof, the inconsistencies one encounters when one takes a stand on issues of life and death, as at times one must.Unfortunately, one cannot always be right.

B. Variations on the Need to Resist

MUNICH

Some Thoughts on Germans and Jews

Written September, 1972

How could it be that Jews once again were allowed to die in Munich, a few miles from Dachau, their hands tied behind their backs, blindfolds on their eyes? And why did only two offer resistance? The rest were not skinny, docile Yeshiva students or helpless women and children. They were tough Israeli Jews who were also prodigious wrestlers, bulky weightlifters and infallible marksmen. How could they have allowed themselves to be killed?

Twenty-eight years have passed since the last Jews were killed at Dachau. That makes twenty-eight years of impassioned denunciation of Jewish passivity in the concentration camps; twenty-eight years of grave admonitions always to remember, never to let it happen again; twenty-eight years of educating Jewish children that one must stand and manfully fight for the right to live, that one must always be on guard.

How is it possible that the Israeli Olympic team was not on guard, that the world-famous Israeli security forces were not adequately prepared for the attack? How come the athletes themselves, most of whom were citizen-soldiers, did not prove more effective defenders of their own lives? All obvious explanations seem palpably insufficient.

Some strong paralyzing, emasculating force must have been at work to allow the Black September Movement success in their atrocious act of terror. They succeeded despite timely warnings of their treacherous intentions, despite the fact that the Olympics were an obvious tempting target for a public spectacle and so should have enjoyed high security, despite the fact that everyone knew Germany contained two thousand Arab students most of whom hate Israel with a vitriolic intensity.

They succeeded because of the absurd relationship between the Germans and Jews, because of the Jew's ambivalent admiration for things German. This Jewish admiration is of a special kind. It is like Kafka's love for his father – intimidating and sometimes totally debilitating, filled with a shuddering and embittering fear, but nonetheless an essential prop for self-understanding and a goad to creativity.

In the past century the ominous admiration of the Jew for the German has manifested itself in three major ways.

The first of these is social and cultural. From the emancipation onward the Jew has respectfully venerated German culture and manners. Although German ways are frequently the butt of Eastern European humor, in the crucial moments it is German cultural-styled leaders who are accepted, followed and venerated by the Eastern European Jews.

It took an Austrian Jew, born in Budapest, with his clean linen, polished urbane style, and impeccable demeanor, to galvanize Jewish national consciousness. Herzl's Germanic way was not an impediment to his endearment to the Jewish masses, as we are generally accustomed to believe. It was instead one of the causes of this endearment. In spite of their ambivalence toward and sense of alienation from all that Herzl represented, the Jewish masses responded positively to the man and to his self-assured authoritative manner. Theodore Herzl is Judaism's abiding symbol of the loving fascination with things German.

Jewish admiration for the Germans is also intellectual. Jews have explored their own collective identity with theories and concepts of personality, society and culture that were Germanic in origin. The first traces of Jewish historical awareness that attempted to be objective were those nurtured by the German intellectual world and by the methodologies developed in that world. Indeed, talking points in the ongoing discussions concerning Jewish historical reality have been those formulated by German-trained Eastern European intellectuals. From Steinschneider's work in bibliographic studies, Graetz's history, Schechter's Rabbinic studies, Heschel's philosophy, and Wellhausen and Ehrlich's work in Bible, modern Jewish humanistic studies have been German in inspiration, method and substance. Jewish self-understanding, insofar as it has a historical dimension, has been mediated by German styles of thought, criteria of truth and institutional structures.

Thirdly Jews have admired German technology and its products. Of course Jews are not alone in their respect for German technology, but with them this respect verges on veneration. How else can one explain the disturbing ubiquity of German goods in Israel, a large proportion of whose people suffered German atrocities. German ships, cars, electronic goods and synthetic fabrics have successfully broken anti-German inhibitions. The attraction has proven stronger than the taboo.

Nonetheless, permeating the strong Jewish emotional attachment to German manners, consciousness and technology is a sense of victimization which brings with it hate and fear. The feelings are complex. There are those who perpetually chronicle Nazi barbarities with dreadful intensity. The zealous hunters of former Nazis who crave vengeance for past abominations have a bitter, brooding quality.

On the other hand public statements from concentration camp survivors are understandably pervaded with a melancholy self pity. And one also finds that macabre aspect of victimization, that psychological reality which is so difficult to justify morally, the identification of the victim with the victimizer, the acceptance by the victim of the evaluation made of him. This mechanism we have seen at work in the concentration camps, in the Korean prison stockades and in urban ghettos. It is at work in particularly virulent form in the ongoing relationship between Jews and Germans.

Israelis have come to accept the superior competence of the Germans, their efficiency, reliability, excellence and resourcefullness. From such acceptance the road is short to a generalized belief in their moral superiority – precisely the type of belief that feelings of victimization feed upon. And the Israeli feeling of victimization through German superiority is reinforced by another important factor – one which compromises a value of Israeli society.

Israelis base their current ethos of self reliance and military self sufficiency on their determination not to be helpless and vulnerable any longer. Never again will the world be allowed to comfortably ignore Jewish suffering; never again will Jews be led to the slaughter like sheep. Israelis have a bitter contempt for the Jews who permitted themselves to be abused without making the Nazis pay dearly. However, this striving for self reliance and rejection of vulnerable dependence have been severely compromised in Israel in two cases. First, Israel depends on America for arms and economic aid; second, it depends on German reparations.

Handling this reality without a perverse psychological reaction has proven difficult. The reliability, efficiency and generosity of German reparations has reinforced beliefs in German moral superiority. Almost two decades have passed since Israel became dependent on German reparations. Thanks to the Germans there has been a steady stream of goods which have benefited tens of thousands of individuals and through them thousands of others. The Israeli government has benefited through direct grants and industrial and cultural projects.

The original justification in Israel for accepting German reparations was the feeling that "we have the right to expect the Germans to take care of us," and "we have suffered long enough, it is coming to us." This need for compensation for past sufferings has led to a feeling of respect and admiration for the prowess of one capable of meeting our needs. These are the very mechanisms that create the phenomenon of victimization everywhere.

It is not beyond the perverse workings of the unconscious that guilt-ridden Israelis should secretly identify with the victimizers of the

Jewish people. Did not the Israeli who wanted to end the diaspora find in the Germans an unintending contributing agent to the creation of the State? Do no Israelis who reject the diaspora stereotype of the Jew find in the Germans the murderous agents who destroyed the human embodiments of that stereotype? It would be grotesque and unacceptable to the conscious mind and sensibilities to find any overt manifestations of these feelings, but the paralyzed Israeli reaction to the Olympic games in Munich seems to offer indirect support of this analysis. Why were the Israelis caught off guard in anticipating the activities of ten Palestinian organizations with 142 branches, 3,000 members and 15 newspapers in Germany?

In Israel, the Munich Olympics were an important event from the start. Israelis were promised excellent coverage of the games. National attention was given to a special dedication ceremony celebrating the completion of a TV satellite transmissions ground station which would bring the games live to the Israeli public. President Nixon, Prime Minister Meir, and leading world figures spoke to the TV audience. The preparations of the athletes for the games, their departure, arrival and participation in the opening festivities were carried live on Israeli TV. Everyone was involved. They were headline material. When Esther Shahamarov failed to qualify for the 100 meter semifinals women's track event, there were audible shouts of disappointment from homes all over Israel. Israel was intensely involved in the games. Why?

One of the reasons was that it was a triumphant demonstration of Jewish normalcy. There was a perverse tone of "we too." We too can value our body; we too can develop our physical capacities so that we can compete internationally; we too can parade; we too can fly our flag. We have physical prowess just like everyone else. For once the tantalizing dream of all Judaism's false prophets seemed to be coming true. For once we were like all other nations.

A frequently overlooked fact about the Jew is his jealousy of others who have children that grow up to be relatively normal. Jewish children, by contrast, tend to become either singular, unprecedented, celebrated legends, or lamentable but heroic failures. In short, Jews have a propensity to become either Messiahs or schlemiels. Where else could the achievement of normalcy be better demonstrated than in the very country where Jews had been singled out for the most abnormal treatment of all – genocide. There was a special sweetness to seeing the Israeli flag paraded on the stadium grounds of Munich. We were being accepted as regular in the very country that treated us most exceptionally.

The new Jew had arrived.

But the Olympic games proved a dramatic, tragic, Jewish-German absurdity from start to finish. The tortured absurdities were many. First the participants. Many of the Israeli participants in the games looked disconcertingly like middle-aged castoffs from European ghettos, while Jewish athletes from other countries, like Mark Spitz and Shane Gould, looked like kibbutzniks with blond hair, mustaches and all.

Next, the sporting specialities of the Israeli team: shooting, wrestling, weight-lifting – these are the characteristics not of Jacob but of Esau. Their blatant Hellenistic overtones do violence to the Jewish historical consciousness. If ever there was *goyim naches,* this was it.

Next, Dachau. Even though the Germans made elaborate preparations for a service at Dachau to honor the Jewish dead, even though hundreds of repentant and respectful Germans attended, only two out of the twenty-seven Israelis saw fit to attend. The Germans were more respectful of the Jewish dead than the Jews themselves. The very dead that the Germans had killed.

Next, the extreme dialectical swing. The Jews were the biggest winners and the biggest losers of the Olympics. Mark Spitz's father seems to have been wrong when he justified not giving his son a Jewish education by saying "Even God likes a winner." Not true when it comes to Jewish hubris. The events seem to be the churlish antics of some malevolent, powerful but petty divinity.

Next, the lack of precautions. The Germans, who had so much to lose from the chronicle of events, who had so much desire to prove their humanistic concern for life to the world, who are generally so efficient and competent, were most incompetent and inefficient when it came to protecting Jewish lives. And Israelis who are invincible on their own soil proved to be totally ineffective when away from it.

Next, no one was himself. Everyone was dressed in someone else's clothes. The German security authorities were dressed like hotel managers; the Arabs were dressed as security authorities; the Jew who escaped and was interviewed on Israeli TV looked like a frightened Arab in pajamas. No one was himself. Germans weren't responsible, Israelis weren't invincible and Arabs weren't cowards.

Next, handling of the news. Israelis glued themselves to their radios the entire day of the events. People gathered around everywhere to find out what was happening. The day dragged on with its heavy tension... the afternoon news... the depressing evening news... 12:00 a.m.... 1:00 a.m. Then, at 1:30, while all Israel was in bed listening to the constant radio reports from Munich, the unexpected miracle was announced. The Israelis had overpowered their captors.

Everyone went to sleep secure in the belief that we had done it again. The morning newspapers carried headlines announcing that the captives were well... and then the depressing truth was announced. No one respects truth as much as the Israeli. For two days quiet music was played on the radio to recover from the double shock of the events themselves and of having believed a lie.

What is it about the Jew that makes every contact with the German tragically and absurdly dramatic? What is it about the Germans that fascinates the Jew yet immobilizes and paralyzes him? The answer, we believe, is that each believes in the other's superiority, and yet at the same time feels like the other's victim. Germans and Jews seem to be locked into a mutually metamorphosing, antipathetic symbiosis.

This symbiosis is not morally based. There is no way of morally condoning Germany's attempt to annihilate the Jewish people. And a Jewish act of self defense is morally defensible. Dachau has no moral justification, Israel has.

Nonetheless, paradoxes and absurdities abound.

By manipulating German and anti-Semitic fears, Hitler came into power. As a result of both the holocaust and Hitler's defeat, the German ceased to be the ideal warrior and became instead the paradigmatic businessman of Europe, while the landless, prudent, Jewish businessman became the intrepid, nationalistic warrior. Germany, originally one of Jewry's greatest friends, allowing citizenship privileges to Jews which few other European countries permitted, became Jewry's most dangerous enemy. And then in its defeat it became the unwilling agent for one of Jewry's greatest achievements – the State of Israel.

And paradoxically, Jews, who had paid German culture the greatest compliment by accepting its superiority and assimilating into it as into no other culture before or since, who became uncompromisingly hostile when it proved so treacherous, ultimately became dependent upon German largesse for their State; a painful rapprochement is being attempted, and is failing.

Munich is only one of a series of absurd events that have linked the German and the Jew. How could the Germans have been so inefficient? How could they have overlooked adequate security? How could they have planned so poorly to handle the Arab terrorists? And once the events began to unfold, how could they fail to keep to their plan? How could German marksmen have been so poor? How could the Israelis have been lulled into accepting German protection? How could they not have taken their own adequate measures? How could they have been so ineffective once the events began to unfold?

There were paralyzing, immobilizing forces at work on both sides. While no inexorable fate requires history to repeat itself tediously, the events at Munich demonstrate that history's influence remains powerful, especially in the relationship between German and Jew.

Between Germans and Jews we have two superior cultures victimizing each other with mutually paralyzing consequences. Memory fails and reasoning is inadequate in the face of such an absurdity.

YOM KIPPUR
A Letter to a Friend
Written January, 1974

Dear Friend,

I hesitate to write to you for fear I will not do justice to the events I have witnessed since the beginning of the Yom Kippur War three and a half months ago. However, I know you would appreciate a first-hand account even though my role in the recent hostilities was certainly peripheral. Seeing things up close is very different from seeing them in a newspaper or on the TV screen, and this is the difference I want to convey to you.

When I heard about the war, as you know, I was in the States, and I flew home as quickly as possible. I did not get to go home. I was taken straight to the army base where assignments are made. I was assigned to the unit that deals with army morale, with rumor, extreme shock, etc. etc. A mixed bag of concerns for a unit made up primarily of University-type psychologists, psychiatrists, and a sprinkling of social workers. I am the only sociologist.

Our first big project was a morale study on the Golan heights and in Syria. For two weeks we were driving around occupied Syria dodging artillery barrages and assorted dangers and having incredible talks with soldiers in almost every conceivable circumstance – on tanks, in them, under them. It was frightening as hell. The full realization of how close the Syrians had come to Rosh Pina hit me only when I saw the burnt out Syrian tanks on the slope down from the Golan Heights. They had overrun most of the bases on the Heights, and were on their way down to the heartland. Their continuing attack was stopped by a mere few dozen officers – most of whom were killed in the process. These officers had gone from one Israeli tank to another shooting the twenty or so artillery shells at the hundreds of Syrian tanks going by. I spoke to one fellow who had taken out fifty Syrian tanks. It would be impossible for me to describe the terror in his eyes when I spoke to him ten days after the event. He swore that he would never go near a tank again.

One day in Syria I found myself on a road called the American Axis. I had made the trip from America but the landscape was like the other side of the moon. Then a Suchoi flew overhead, and the soldiers around me opened up with everything they had. The plane was only about forty yards off the ground and the group managed to bring it down. The death of the pilot seemed just another small event in the general insanity. I discovered that I am capable of killing, and I find it a strange and upsetting discovery. There was a time not so very long ago when I was committed to non-violence.

After our experience in Syria, we were ordered down to Egypt. In the weeks that followed I crossed over into Egypt five times, but the first crossing was overwhelming. We were in a tender and there was shelling. The closer we got to the bridges the more I wanted to get the hell out of there. The imminence of death brings everyone's senses to a very fine focus. As we got closer and closer I said to myself – there is still time to jump off; what am I doing here? It's absolutely crazy going into Egypt; who wants to be there in the first place? I had climbed onto the roof of the tender with my helmet on and the Uzi hanging from my shoulder. From my perch I could see everything. Everywhere we saw terrible signs of the Egyptian army's efficiency. Scores of burnt-out tanks lay around. the ground was covered with shell cases and burnt trucks, most of them our own. But my first strong impression was from the smell of the sea right in the middle of the desert. The bitter lake, which joins the canal, is a sizable body of water, and our bridges are built where the canal joins the bitter lake. What impressed me the most was the sea breeze. If one could feel the sea, then things couldn't be all that bad.

As we crossed over I felt totally exposed, terribly vulnerable. I never thought we would make it across those creaky pontoons. We weren't more than a few yards across on the other side when I saw my first corpse... and then another and another. At first I tried to tell myself that they were not people but big dolls. I found it unacceptable to think of those puffed up things in soldier's clothing as anything more than specimens from Madame Toussaud's wax collection. And then the smell hits you. I had never really smelled death before. I kept thinking of *The Brothers Karamazov* and the astonishment of the monks when Father Zossima's body begins to rot. The smell is powerful... powerful. It is pungent and hauntingly, strangely sweet. In a way it is comforting because it is only right that the death of a human being should leave a powerful reminder. Egyptian bodies were being "buried" by bulldozers since the Egyptians had indicated that they did not want their dead soldiers back.

The dogs in Egypt did not go hungry during the war. Everywhere we went we saw scores of dogs digging up corpses, eating parts of human bodies. As one cynical soldier said, "the only thing the dogs want from the Israelis are pickles to eat with their meat."

At first we spoke to soldiers in the Ismailia area, where we came under a murderous katyusha attack. Fortunately I found a student of mine (one who had gotten good grades from me), and he showed me a wonderfully deep hole in the ground. I rolled myself up into the smallest ball possible and promptly fell asleep. Through the night I incorporated the noise around me into my dreams as I slept. For the first time in my life I felt every heartbeat. I became intimately connected with inner physical processes. I couldn't get over the fact that my heart was skipping beats in coordination with the sound of shells falling – and all this while I was in a semi-stupor. There is absolutely nothing an individual can do against an artillery attack except be afraid, become small, go down deep. That was me. An irregular heartbeat, deep down in the sand.

We got up the next morning in a desert mist, quickly burned off by the sun. Suddenly, out of nowhere, Yoram Gaon appeared. He is the Dean Martin of the Israeli entertainment world, and he had come to sing and tell jokes. Boy did I sing and laugh. It seems macabre, but that is what happened. Everything else is absurd so why not enjoy it? Benjamin Nelson has an essay on the Dance of Death. It is so true that the impulse to dance is strongest when death is closest. Laughter, song, bodily vigor are a natural response to danger.

As I went around speaking to tank crews and asking them what they had done while they were riding off to battle, their answers further confirmed what I had felt. The response I heard most often was "We sang, of course." There had been times when five of our tanks rode out to battle forces of a hundred enemy tanks. I don't know what the Arab tank crews were doing at the time, but imagine if they were also singing. Men killing each other in the most ghastly ways, and all the while singing.

When the ceasefire day approached, everyone felt a special sense of danger. The relief one feels at the possibility of an end to all the hell is eclipsed by the fear of dying during the last moments of the fighting. The feelings of invulnerability which enable one to function start to wear off and one is left with more realistic feelings of fear that deepen and spread as the hour draws near. The hour of 7:00 p.m. had been chosen for the start of the ceasefire, and at 6:55 the Egyptians let loose with every gun they had. It was then one saw fear unadulterated by false illusions.

There was no ceasefire... and the fire had not ceased.

As I write we are still at war. As long as any soldier is killed – and almost a hundred have been killed since the formal ceasefire – everyone is still at war. Every day on all the fronts there are exchanges of artillery and small arms fire.

After the October 22nd agreement our unit concentrated its efforts on shell shock and battle fatigue. These terms don't begin to describe the situation. The diversity of symptoms is staggering. On the one hand there are people in a semi-catatonic state, and on the other there are the hyper-active shakers and pacers. It is pathetic to see. We slept in the psychiatric ward of the shock treatment center in the southern war zone, and every night we overheard the sleeping soldiers cry out in their sleep. One would shout "They are coming!" and another would answer "Quick, fire from all weapons."

Fully ten percent of all casualties were shell shock. The number of casualties, including dead and wounded, is now around 11,000. When all the "missing" are certified as dead by the army rabbinate, there will be close to 3,000 dead. A major disaster by anyone's count. My secretary's husband was killed, a number of my students, the brother of one of my department colleagues, etc. etc. In order to get an analogous picture of the impact on American society you would have to multiply by seventy or so, but even then the whole story would not be conveyed because of the difference in societal structure and interconnections.

It is now January, 1974. I am still in the army, but we got some time off to relax and decompress. We are all under enormous stress and it is a welcome relief to unwind. Today I managed to open my last letter from the summer pile. It seems incredible that there were letters from August still unopened.

As you have no doubt concluded, this has been a miserable war. The most amazing part is that people here seem still prepared for whatever is in store despite the heavy price paid. No one wants the hostilities to resume, and there is a spirit of reasonableness in the air, but people are determined not to be caught off guard again, and also not to be pressured into a peace settlement which is suicidal. Israel remains strong, and if the Arabs are interested in peace they will find many friends in Israel willing to work for it. However, if it is war they want, we are more ready than before.

The recent elections here witnessed a strengthening of both the right and the left. In my view, that is as it should be. We must be both tough and conciliatory. It seems to me we are about to make conciliatory gestures to the Arabs, but the future of the peace depends on their responses.

I have not yet finished serving with my army unit, and the existential reality and meaning of these few months is too fresh to put into focus. Somewhere, however, there is a pattern of meaning that connects together my involvements in Selma, Alabama, my anti-Vietnam War work, and my service in the Israeli army. In the meantime I will leave it to you to make the synthesis. I hope to see you soon. Come and see us in Haifa... it's the loveliest part of Israel. We have mountains, forests, and most of all, the sea.

Gene

LEBANON

A Letter From Israel

Written September, 1982

Dear Kate and Carol,

I am presuming to write to you together rather than separately since, quite frankly, I don't know if I can deal individually with the issues you raise (where does one get the strength?) Besides, there is a great deal of overlap in all our concerns.

First, the bare facts of personal experience that inform my attitudes. When the war broke out three months ago, on June 6th, I was in a kind of summer doldrum – more precisely, a Haifa-induced summer calm, one filled with clear colors, breezy days and Carmel chirpings. David was around, Carolyn's presence was a pleasant addition, and things were wonderfully sleepy.

Danny, Mindy, David and Carolyn went to see the movie *Gallipoli* on Saturday night. We babysat. I have always regarded *Gallipoli* as a fascinating battle. There was Churchill, of all people, sending tens of thousands of men to die in a useless, stupid battle fought with incompetence and ill-defined goals, and yet Churchill the politician and statesman survives. He not only survives after being discredited and going into exile of sorts, he is called back to serve his country. The Hitler period required an English leader who didn't flinch and could send men to their death over goals he defined to be in the national interest.

They came back from the movie minus Danny. Coming out of the theatre they had seen groups of young men waiting for transportation to report to their army units. Danny didn't wait to be called up to his paratrooper unit. He went with them to be dropped off at his base.

After the Argov shooting in London, the Israel bombing attack and the PLO shelling of Nahariya and the Galillee, it was inevitable that something big would happen, but we had not guessed what. And here it was. Danny had gone. Danny always tells us not to wonder about where he is if there is any military action... his unit will be the first on the front line.

And indeed that is the way it happened. Danny's unit went through our Ahuza neighborhood early Sunday morning. Tanks, personnel carriers, thousands of beautiful guys and all. Because of the size of the country there is no space between the military and the civilian, and war takes on a comprehensive quality. The tanks go through your neighborhood to get to the front, and the front is only an hour away. The juxtaposition of mothers with infants in carriages and this machinery of war was overwhelming. A number of times I saw guys waving to their wives or neighbors as they went by. The pathos of the scene was unforgettable. Especially powerful for me was the age spread of the men. It was approximately from eighteen to forty.

By Sunday night Danny was in Lebanon fighting his way up the coast. All day Sunday we sat around in a kind of stupor with the radio on all the time, reassuring one another that somehow it wouldn't be too bad, but not believing a word we were saying. I slept with the radio on all night. By Monday morning the battle reports started coming in and it was clear that a lot of people were getting killed. I reported to my army unit, the psychological unit, and requested to be sent into Lebanon to work with the severe casualties. One of my closest friends, Reuven Gal, is the Colonel in charge of the unit and he said he was going there as well. Tuesday morning he picked me up in an army car and we headed into Lebanon.

In order to get in we had to go through Kiryat Shmoneh. The population there was in the streets in front of their shelled houses throwing candies, and handing cakes and drinks to the army cars. There was a lot of weeping. After the events of last summer when many had to live in shelters for weeks at a time because of the constant PLO shelling, they were finally getting the protection they had been begging for. Any soldier who went through Kiryat Shmoneh during the first days of the war went into battle with a sense of certainty that he was fighting a *just war*. The relief on the faces of those civilians was too palpable to be faked. Their joy was not the joy of war hysteria, but more like "I am so glad you are here to protect us now."

It turned out that the car we were in was considered by army standards a "soft vehicle," and there were standing orders that they were not allowed into Lebanon. We had to leave our car and hitchhike for the next week on personnel carriers and trucks. Still we traveled all over Lebanon. We went with the troops wherever they were going and had a chance to see the war very close up – sometimes too close for comfort. All along we were doing what we were there for, talking to the men, asking questions – How do you feel about what you are doing? What have you been through? How are you holding up? We spoke to dozens of soldiers of every sort in a great variety of circumstances. After a number of days we reported back and found we had information which individuals at the highest levels of command wanted desperately. We felt that in addition to being of service to soldiers in the field we were also having an impact on the planning process.

Basically, what emerged from our talks with men in the field was their anxiety over the question of "limits." The Israeli military machine is so powerful when you see it up front that it seems to be capable of doing almost anything. When the London Institute of Strategic Studies listed us fourth in the world in military capability behind the U.S.A., Russia and China, it did not come as a surprise to anyone who saw what we are capable of. It is awesome. Frightening as hell, but awesome. Israelis, by temperament and socialization, always are prepared to "go to the end" in any confrontation. Well, here was a war with no natural end and it was very anxiety-provoking. Where do you stop the damn thing?

Concretely, the soldiers in their black humorous way talked about being issued a world globe instead of the secret coded maps that field units are given of the area in which they will be operating. Older reservists nicknamed Sharon "Gringo" as in the Viva Zapata movie – fast on the draw and itching for a fight. Everyone knows that Sharon is a military genius, but there is a great suspicion that he lacks self-imposed limits.

On one of our trips back to report in Israel, we were called to meet with the psychiatric and psychological staff of a very large hospital receiving army wounded. It was midnight. The emergency room was the size of a basketball court. There were two to three hundred doctors and nurses working in teams to save the lives of scores of wounded soldiers who had been helicoptered in. Language in these situations is intrinsically euphemistic. "Badly wounded" means without legs, arms, more. The guys we were with had been whole, healthy young men in the flush of youthful exuberance and now were wrecks, hulks, pathetic helpless human beings trying to preserve a semblance of humanity.

The psychological staff there to deal with the shock of the soldiers, doctors, medical personnel, parents, spouses, siblings and friends of the wounded were on the verge of collapse. Reuven and I spent a good part of the night and the next day just trying to keep the shock of the staff within limits so that they could continue to function. All that was needed was to talk and to listen. In such a situation, people search for anyone in the group who is not overwhelmed by anxiety. If you are relatively composed, for whatever reason – and I mean *really* composed and not just faking it – that communicates. There seems to be a contagion effect to composure just as there is a contagion effect to panic and hysteria – especially among those who have socially defined roles as helpers and support people.

I was in a position to know at all times exactly where Danny's unit was fighting. The casualty and killed lists were available to me at most times and I, of course, looked as often as I could. Thank God I never found his name. But names there were, and some were people I knew and from families I know. Three hundred and fifty dead as I write, and I know three of them, and their families. That "knowledge" makes it very difficult for the Israeli to relate seriously to the world of "TV images" that constitutes "knowledge" for the American. (More on this point later on.)

All in all we spent two months in Lebanon through all phases of the war. The situation changed over the period and the soldiers' attitudes changes. Strangely enough my basic attitudes have not changed. In contrast to both Danny and David who emerged rather critical about this war and ambivalent about the part they played in it, I did not. When David was assigned to an artillery unit on the Beirut-Damascus road, and Danny was sitting on a hill overlooking Beirut, it was very, very difficult for me as a father. As the weeks went by I kept asking myself "Would you be so sure that this is a just war if something happened to Danny or David?" "Is what we are gaining by destroying the infrastructure of the PLO worth anyone's life?" That is the bottom line question. "Is it worth it?"

The war began three months ago. At no point in the whole business did I ever feel in doubt about whether it was worth it. For me that is a "first" in my life because I always see the other side and it frequently seems plausible. Here I was participating in something about which I had and still have moral certainty. I think it was the right thing for us to go into Lebanon given the circumstances; I am glad we did it, and furthermore, I think the long-range effects are going to be positive for us and for the Palestinians.

My reasoning:

This whole operation cannot be judged simply by the intentions of the principals. It is clear that Sharon and Begin are interested in removing the military threat of the PLO so that they can have a freer hand in the West Bank. Their position is the Israeli version of the Gunboat Diplomacy – Monroe Doctrine – Dominate the Bastards – A good Indian is a Dead Indian American precedents. But as Hegel has taught us, one's intention when in a position of power, and the outcome of one's actions, are separate entities. Unintended consequences, paradoxical effects, ironies, counter-productive dynamics and the like all have their impact. In moral calculus, we must consider the outcome of action. I do not say that intentions count for nothing in the equation, but they are not the primary factor. Does anyone who has anything to do with psychology have to be reminded that "Love is not Enough?" Not in child rearing, marriage or even in a love relationship between one's children.

My general reaction to someone who wants to do something for me is to run for my life. The good intention usually is the beginning of disaster.

Can anyone doubt that today, three months after the war, a Palestinian state is nearer to being realized than at any time in the past? That Begin and Sharon's policy has given greater legitimacy to the plight of the Palestinian people than at any time in the past?

Because of this war the stage is set for any evolutionary process that will bring peace to the Middle East. First, Begin and Sharon have transformed American policy from passive participation to active involvement in the PLO issue. The world now wants a solution to this problem, and the PLO is finding friends everywhere. Second it has been Israel's responsibility to demonstrate to the PLO forcibly and relentlessly that they cannot have the whole cake, but will have to settle for less, and that they cannot *take it* but will have to negotiate in a give and take. The decline in the PLO's military power and ascendance of their moral power opens that door. Before, when the PLO was militarily powerful there was no possibility for any compromise with them. Why should they compromise as long as there was a possibility of dominating Lebanon and the West Bank by the use of the military threat. But as victims of Israeli "ruthlessness," the PLO can now base their political appeal on moral superiority. If they play that right, and all signs seem to be that Arafat is cooling the hotheads, they will have more confidence in a political solution.

Further, I believe that if Hussein came to Jerusalem now he would get the same kind of enthusiastic reception as Sadat. I also believe that if Arafat unilaterally renounced the use of force and led a peace march to the Israeli frontier using passive resistance, he would get the West Bank. The stage is now set, in my estimation, for a grand gesture by a master statesman. Israel under military threat is one Israel, but once convinced that the other side is genuinely willing to live in peace, Israel will react differently. Oh yes, there are the Israeli ideologues who want the West Bank and more for historical reasons, but I believe they constitute a minority in this country. The West Bank is important to most Israelis primarily because of the security issue. A PLO that renounces violence is a PLO transformed, a PLO that radically redefines the security situation; even Begin and Sharon would have to recognize that.

Now to respond to your statement, Kate, that American Jews feel betrayed. I have long felt that the perception of Israel by people outside of Israel, and particularly by Israel's friends, suffers from strong doses of idealization and mystification. What do these concepts mean? An unwillingness to accept the reality of things. Israel, in the minds of many (including its most intimate supporters and friends), is still not an accomplished fact. Israel's existence is regarded as shaky and tenuous. There is something about the Zionist accomplishment which defies easy, unquestioned acceptance. And I see a direct connection between the perception of the Jew, due to the influence of Christian theology over the centuries, and the current perceptions of Israel.

In regard to Israel, most people (including many Jews) feel that essence precedes, and is morally superior to, existence. That is simply not so. Israel exists and will continue to exist. She will not "go down the drain" as the current bathroom (or is it kitchen?) metaphor has it. The country is relatively united about most of the fundamental issues. The Eli Geva controversy, the reluctance of some armed men to go to Beirut and their willingness to say it publicly during a time of war is an important indicator of Israeli democracy.

For the people of the Book, the prototypical humanists, the idealistic, pioneer socialists, to bomb Beirut in order to get at the PLO is a moral scandal. But the bombing of Beirut was a moral scandal only if judged by essentialistic criteria. A good country does not do such a thing. A good country perhaps should continue to allow itself to be shelled by those who have sworn to destroy it?

The fact that Israel was determined not to let the PLO use civilians to hide behind has been a consistent policy of all Israel's governments – and it has not mattered whether those civilians are Jews or non-Jews, adults or children. One simply cannot let an adversary who has sworn to destroy you use innocent people as a shield when attacking. There is no way out of that moral dilemma aside from going in after the adversary "no matter what."

What Israel is all about is the simple fact that the Jew has entered history again – or at least twenty percent of the world's Jews. We finally have to be responsible as Jews for collecting our own garbage and running our own jails. For two thousand years we have let the *goyim* do that. We have been alternatively the *luftmenshen* and the small capitalists, sitting back and criticizing, projecting utopias while our hands remained pure, and left the grimy nitty gritty for the others.

Jews have been innocent of atrocity for two thousand years. There is no Jewish Grand Inquisitor, no Attila the Hun, no bloodthirsty bastards who have succeeded in doing terrible things to large groups of people. Not that these types did not exist, or that their sentiments were not publicly declared. In the Jewish prayerbook – or the Passover Haggadah or the Book of Esther – there is plenty of anger expressed at the *goyim*. It was just that it was too dangerous to let these sentiments escape into the realm of action. They remained just sentiments for the most part.

Now the Jew is right smack in the middle of history with all sorts of ways to express anger that can really hurt people. The distance between responsibility for actual happenings and moral evaluation has narrowed, that is, for the Jews of Israel. Jews in the diaspora, in this sense, are only part-time Jews. The *goyim* fight the wars in Vietnam and commit terrible crimes but it is the Jews who are the guardians of values. This bifurcation is only possible when one is not responsible for everything. There is always an "out." The Indians? Killed before my grandfather came to America on a steerage ticket. The exploitation of dependent foreign counties by multinational American corporations? What do you want from me, all I have is a few hundred stocks in IBM, and besides, I'm selling them, that makes me an exploiter? The CIA's involvement in El Salvador? Whoever heard of a Jew in the CIA?

As you know, there is no "out" for the Jew in Israel. We are smack in the middle of history where we have no place to go to evade the full responsibility for everything. We are embodied in a particularly lethal institution, the nation state, which for better or worse is the current epidermis of our ragtag religious-cultural-ethical consciousness. It is our current way of being-in-the-world.

Nationhood requires acts that are not always gentlemanly. America is so big, with enough booming, buzzing confusion going on all the time; Americans do not have to face the brutal facts of nationhood. In Israel there is no way of escaping the brutalizing costs of an ongoing, accomplished nationhood and nationalism – particularly in the dangerous situation in which we find ourselves. It is a dirty, brutal world out there, and many people out there do not think well of us – to put it mildly. The big question is how to stand up to brutality without being brutalized oneself.

It has become increasingly difficult for me to engage in the discussion of this central question with American Jews. American Jewish consciousness is so contaminated with the images of the media, and the internalized evaluations of that all-important reference group "the non-Jew," that I sometimes feel there is no one in the States to talk to. By that I mean someone who is willing to confront reality as it is lived in Israel. When American Jews come here to discuss Israel's problems, they are really talking about their own problems of maintaining self-respect. They just call it Israel's problems. Do not think it is so easy to find people here to discuss these issues with. As you know, it is not. Here, we are so close to the hard reality that it is difficult to move away, to see it from a perspective. It is like a book held up to one's nose, so that it is hard for the eyes to focus. That is why, dear friends, I loved your letters. Even though you are "there" you are trying, as we all are, to see things empathetically.

I guess the bottom line of what I am saying to you both is that after three months of this hell... it may even turn out to be good. Who knows?

Gene

NINE MONTHS AFTER LEBANON
A Response to an American Friend
February 26, 1983

Dear Kate,

Thanks for your letter. It has forced me, once again, to define for myself where I stand on the issues you raise. I look forward to continuing the discussion when you come visit on Pesach.

In the meantime, my response:

As usual, I'll start with something immediate. Danny and Mindy just returned from a trip to Egypt. Even though Mindy is in her seventh month of pregnancy, they spent a week traveling on a small pelucca up the Nile, and each day riding around on donkeys among the villages along the river. In most places they were the first Israelis the villagers had met. Everywhere it was the same. They were greeted warmly, and felt tremendous good will. That good will resulted from Sadat's visit to Israel.

Sadat's visit is the most significant event to happen in this part of the world during the past decade. I know many claim that the hawkish, 'jingoistic,' 'imperialistic,' 'expansionist' government of Begin responded to Sadat's overture and braved a virtual civil war within Israeli society over Sinai only because it and its party had no ideological stake in the place. They claim that peace with Egypt seemed to Begin a good military strategy and that it was useful for ultimately annexing the West Bank. But these explanations of why and how Begin and company were willing and able to pull it off miss the one important point. The Israeli people really want peace.

There is undeniable force in Israeli public opinion that wants an end to all the bloodshed in the middle east. Have you forgotten the electric response here to Sadat's visit? I believe the response would be the same for *any* Arab leader willing to declare unambiguously a policy of peace and to back it up with a treaty and normalization procedures. That includes Arafat, Assad and Kadafi. You may think this is an idle, unrealistic fantasy. But I think not.

Sadat's contemptible surprise attack at Yom Kippur cost the lives of 3,000 young Israeli men, as well as 100,000 Egyptians. Yet his visit managed to erase the bitterness and motivate peace-loving people on both sides. Sadat's overture and Begin's response proved that there is a powerful momentum to peace initiatives. They have a logic of their own. The same hawkish Israeli leaders who claimed they would never give away the strategic depth of Sinai for a piece of paper did so willingly after Sadat actually came in person.

Sadat managed to get virtually everything he wanted because he was willing to take a chance for peace. Even the most fanatic Israeli maximalist could see it. It was palpable, believable, and demanded a response on the same high level of morality. The Israelis certainly responded in kind. It was a response to Sadat the person and to his desire for peace.

Why is this important? There are some factors so significant that they create the context within which all else is perceived and experienced. Sadat created a peace context, and within this new context actions suddenly were possible which previously were thought impossible.

Nothing of the sort applies at present with any of the other Arab countries. We are in a formal state of war with all of them, and they have declared their intention to destroy us. They say so, and they act accordingly. The Palestinian National Council has rejected any kind of conciliatory plan, including Reagan's. Indeed they would not let Issam Sartawi even present a case for moderation. And for this state of affairs you imply that Israel is responsible.

By weakening the military potential of the PLO, you say, we are preventing them from being strong enough to compromise; by not recognizing them as the Palestinian people's legitimate leadership we are preventing any meaningful discussion between the sides; by insisting that the PLO is fundamentally a terrorist organization we are denying the legitimacy of Palestinian nationalism; by not waiting for the PLO to gather sufficient military strength to do us great harm, by going after them on our own terms, we are callous to the human tragedy of the Palestinian people, etc. etc.

I do not deny we have our share of crazies who want wars with the Arabs, who want Israel to be a Sparta, who advocate an expansionist

Israel, who think in Oded Yinon's terms. Every country has them and as long as war is the context of reality these people will have their say, and a big say at that. But my God, didn't any PLO leader see the way the population here in Israel responded to the peace initiative of Sadat? Doesn't anyone understand what it took out of this country to give up the Sinai?

Kate, everything I wrote in my original letter to you was predicated on the reality that we have real live enemies out there who want us dead, who don't acknowledge our legitimate existence, and who are preparing for the day of our destruction. Under these conditions I am glad there are people like Eitan and Sharon on our side, just as Americans can be pleased that they had a Patton and a McArthur during World War II. However, should conditions change and a possibility for peace arise, these are the people who must be got rid of, just as Patton and Churchill were deposed after World War II, and McArthur after the Korean War ended.

You say you found in your study that 95 percent of Palestinians recognize the existence of Israel. This does not change the fact that the PLO is committed to its destruction. All it says to me is that if the PLO leadership declared for peace and compromise they would, maybe, have support among the people. So I ask you, as I ask my Arab friends, why don't the Arab leaders come and renounce war as an instrument of policy? Why do they not renounce it as a means for solving problems in the Middle East? Without relinquishing a single one of the demands they regard as just, why don't they come and reason with us, negotiate, talk, pressure us morally, politically, and try to influence the progressive elements in our society? *This is what Sadat did, and in so doing he realized virtually all of what he sought!*

They don't come and they don't negotiate because they have other thoughts in mind. It is they who want an *imposed* settlement, not us. They do not recognize negotiation as a desirable process because they do not recognize our right to negotiate. To this you write: "But why should one party in a conflict have such a right while the other has no say, no freedom to designate its own representatives, its own negotiators?" The answer to your rhetorical question is that it has to be that way. The Arabs start negotiations with tremendous assets. They have Russia on their side, western oil interests, twenty-one Arab countries, one hundred and eighty million or so Arabs around the world, the sympathy of the Third World, the wealth of Croesus. You want us to negotiate with them when there is a situation of military parity? Are you kidding Kate? They don't want to talk to us now because they have not brought us to our knees and we will talk back.Imagine 3 million Jews talking back to 180 million, a country the size of New Jersey with the population of Chicago talking back to the Truth, Justice and The Wave of the Future, to the Oriental Who Has Rediscovered Self-Respect, etc. The gates of Jerusalem are open to all Arab leaders, once they do what Sadat did and proclaim to their own people that Israel is a fact, war is not a solution, legitimate rights must be demanded peacefully.

The solution to the Palestinian problem seems so very obvious. The Palestinian people must have both a homeland and sovereignty – sovereignty achieved incrementally and under conditions which prohibit military activity. Any PLO leader who rejects incrementalism and demilitarization *a priori* is an enemy of the Palestinian people, for the only way Israel will agree to a Palestinian State on the West Bank is on the basis of these two conditions.

And Begin's autonomy offer is the most radical breakthrough the PLO has had. The fact that they do not take Begin at his offer is a most incredible irony of contemporary history. Every right winger I know in Israel is terrified that the autonomy plan will lead inexorably to a Palestinian state. Shmuel Katz's articles in *The Jerusalem Post* following the Camp David accord are an eloquent expression of this fear.

So why doesn't the PLO leadership renounce the use of force and declare themselves open to negotiation? Why Kate? It is because they want the 'whole cake' and think it is within their grasp. They believe any agreement with us is illegitimate, because we have no right to exist as a sovereign nation in a land historically ours.

I defend the Lebanese war in the same way I imagine an Egyptian would defend the Yom Kippur war. It was a tragic necessity that has helped to create a process of useful, positive change. We are at a crucial point in this process. If Reagan, Hussein, Habib, Jemayal and Saudi Arabia can get it all together we just might see a breakthrough. Although the results of the PNC were discouraging, I am convinced by Herb Kelman's analysis and by other reports that Arafat is coming around. If only everyone would come to the negotiating table. The next few months look very ominous if they don't, particularly with the Syrians. The world is in great danger if Syrian air defenses are being coordinated in Russia with the use of Russian satellites.

We only have a few years here to work on these problems. After that the nuclear factor will make all solutions improbable!

You made some comments on nationalism and its attendant dangers, and I agree for the most part. There is, nonetheless, an interesting irony. Many of those who argue in favor of the most rabid, militaristically dominated nationalisms such as that of the Palestinians, are themselves bitter opponents of nationalistic ideologies in their own countries. Americans who support the PLO feel somehow protected from direct confrontation with the evil that is done in the name of American interests and American nationalism – that is, in their name. They manage to benefit from the spoils of American predatory nationalism which is wasting the resources of this world, and yet do not see these benefits as an expression of their own values. They then further compound the irony by championing the nationalism of others in the name of humanitarianism, of course. They then tend to feel quite good about the whole thing, indeed rather morally superior. What they deny in theory they benefit from and protest against those whom they define as victimized. The issue of nationalism is never quite faced squarely.

I think you will agree with me that nationalism is one of the lesser human sentiments. It is rather in the category of tribalism, ethnocentrism, xenophobia – everything we were brought up to disdain. When I described Danny's unit going through Ahuza on the way to the Lebanese front, it was not the "nationalistic spirit" or the "idealistic vision of Israel" that I wished to convey. There was definitely no "parading solemnly" or anything of that kind. Going through Ahuza was the shortest route from the army base to the frontier, and what I saw was Shmulik, half dressed, jumping out the jeep to kiss his wife and Aryeh shouting to someone in the street to tell his wife that he is alright. It was no patriotic vision, but the pathos of husbands, fathers, individuals forced by circumstances to go out and fight.

Nationalism is a sentiment of questionable value. I have nothing but disdain for all uncompromising nationalists, including the Palestinian nationalists. I sense a kind of "ultimate good" quality in the belief many people seem to have in Palestinian nationalism. Should a Palestinian state ever be created it will be as morally suspect and probably as noxious and dangerous as other nation states. The nation state is not a solution, it is the problem. You can say, Kate, that this is all well and good for me to say as an Israeli. After all we have a State, while the Palestinians do not. My reply to this is that Jewish nationalism is generated out of, sustained by, and alas seems to perpetuate, collective tragedy. Nationalism for the Jew is our strategy of last resort. We have tried everything else and found it lacking. We arrived at nationalism filled with ambivalence, partial rejection and fundamental doubt. The fanatic screams of Begin and his minions are first and foremost addressed to their own doubts, and it is precisely these doubts which may save us.

My doubts about nationalism and the nation state, however, in no way inhibit me when it comes to defending Jewish lives or ensuring the security of this place. Too often the enemies of the Jewish people have used our own moral scruples against us. My doubts and reservations about the moral supremacy of the nation state are put in abeyance the moment someone points a gun in the direction of Jews. The Palestinian people may be abused victims, but they question the legitimacy of the only place on earth where the Jewish people can determine their own fate. I feel for the Palestinians. We share a brotherhood of victimization.

Should they come in peace to negotiate their legitimate rights they will find many in Israel responsive and willing to share in the battle for their rightful recompense for what they have lost. The justice they seek, the cause they espouse will find advocates in this country if they give up their role as the Trojan State. If they relinquish their absolutist claims and find more pragmatic, compromising positions, then the work of reconciliation can be started. If not, there will be more dying. The Jewish people have come too long a way in history to be duped into self-destructive acts of pseudo-humanitarianism. There is no way for us to satisfy the PLO under their present terms without committing suicide. This we will not do.

You raise the issue of having convictions from afar. I do not believe that solidarity with whatever Israeli leaders define as good is a *moral* requirement. Begin apparently conveyed such a message to Schindler. This would be the surrender of a moral autonomy which needs to be maintained under *all* possible circumstances. Aside from his own judgement, what else does a person ultimately have? Demanding that a person give up their moral autonomy is one of those dehumanizing acts that can only bring disaster. Nonetheless, there is a moral dilemma involved which needs to be addressed.

The worth of convictions, as convictions, is partially determined by their cost to those who hold them. By "worth" I mean usefulness, capacity to serve as a standard for others and the like. In my mind, convictions are beliefs that are earned in some fashion. Timerman's Argentine convictions have cost him dearly and are earned in ways that his Israel convictions are not. This does not make his Israel convictions wrong, of course, only *relatively* unearned. In point of fact, both sets of convictions and his ability to portray them have made him a wealthy man. There is, however, an important point that separates Timerman from Schindler. Timerman is here. He is willing to bear the consequences of his convictions more directly than Schindler. Again, this does not make Timerman right and Schindler wrong. It just makes Timerman's convictions seem more warranted and of greater worth. I have more respect for Timerman's wrong convictions than Schindler's right convictions, because Timerman is here.

The same goes for you, I might add. The reason for these letters is that I feel your participation, involvement, and deep stake in the events going on here. Your letters speak volumes about how much you are "here." But with all your knowledge and firsthand experience, your convictions are relatively unearned. So if you plan to hold them, or use them as a basis for a career, you must put yourself more on the line by being here. After all, the convictions you hold about the Lebanese war have been formed without direct contact with the events themselves – here! And here includes Lebanon, of course.

To be perfectly frank, I suspect the corrupting influence of commercial success on Timerman's convictions, and I also suspect the academic environment in the States (including Harvard). I doubt their capacity for relatively unprejudiced reflection about our problems, and certainly their willingness to permit the Zionist position a sympathetic hearing. In such an intellectual environment I believe it would be virtually impossible for you to maintain your objectivity. I read *The Chronicle of Higher Education* and see that the atmosphere on the campuses concerning Israel is anti-Semitic, and I use the word advisedly.

And so, Kate, we all have our problems focusing on the reality out there. We are all part of our environments. The responsible way to continue studying the issues is the way you have done until now, first hand, on the line, person to person, questioning, probing, evaluating, analyzing and looking from many different perspectives. Do come for Pesach and get to see how things look again, now, at this point in time, from over here.

Looking forward to your visit. We send our love to you.

Gene

C. Resisting Violence:
Danny Timerman's Conscientious Objection

Written October, 1982

4:30 in the morning on October 19th, 1982, my wife Anita said to me, "you have to do something for the Timermans." I was sound asleep and heard the words very faintly. They were indistinguishable from my dream, and I rolled deeper under the covers, trying to sink into the dream. "I said you really must do something for the Timermans." It was useless to try to fight it; it wasn't working.

I got up, made coffee, went downstairs for *Haaretz* and *The Jerusalem Post*, and came up reading and drinking. While I was in the middle of the lead article Anita said to me, "you have to do something about Danny Timerman."

"What the hell could I do."

Danny Timerman in an army prison! It was an unbelievably stupid thing for the Israeli military to jail a wonderful, apolitical guy. He decided he didn't want to be an army policeman in Lebanon searching civilians for arms. It was understandable why he didn't want to do it. His father was tortured by police, How could he be a policeman?

Danny Timerman is a committed Zionist and a Kibbutz member. He is married to a fourth generation Sabra. He volunteered for the Israeli army even though he didn't have to; he served as a sapper during the Lebanese war in the summer of '82 and was due to be released from army service in less than eight days when he was jailed for not wanting to serve in Lebanon. Sentenced to twenty-eight lousy days in an army jail. What a stupid move.

Jacobo Timerman, the *Darkness at Noon* Argentinian Jew, and his son the Israeli counterpart. The media will have a ball with this one.

It is a melodramatic measure-for-measure proof that the Jew is at root everything the antiSemites are accused of being. I can just see all the news editors licking their chops. The intrinsic drama of it. Why couldn't the Israeli army just let Danny Timerman wash dishes for eight days in Israel's Oshkosh and try to forget the whole thing. How many Israeli soldiers' families were tortured the way the Timermans were for three years in Buenos Aires? How many Israeli soldiers have fathers that can get their story in the *New Yorker* magazine, *The New York Times,* and have TV interviews on NBC, CBS and BBC on the same day? Hasn't Israel taken enough of a media beating in the last few months? This too we need? What am I supposed to do? Who do you think I am, the Lone Ranger or something?

Maybe it was because Anita wouldn't let me read the newspaper, my morning dose of history which I need, I must have, in order to start the day, but by 5:45 I found myself on the phone calling Zalman,

"What is the matter?" he asked.

"Nothing, I just want to know how I can get in the army jail in Atlit to see an army prisoner."

He didn't ask me why I called so early in the morning. It was if he was accustomed to calls like mine. I wondered if he got many of them because of who he is, a social worker in the psychiatric unit of the Israeli Army. On second thought, I concluded that, indeed, he must get many calls like mine. Strange country.

"You need to get permission from the Chief Army Officer of Haifa," he said flatly. Somehow I hadn't thought of doing that. It was the obvious answer, since the Chief Army Officer of Haifa is the liaison with all the army jails. A reserve officer like myself in the psychological division should have known that. I knew Beno the officer in charge; in fact I was even working with him on several problems and was on standby for his calls.

I went to see Beno about 9:30. I figured that since I do some occasional work for him and his staff I had a good chance of getting his permission. Furthermore, during the war in Lebanon I had helped him deal with a special problem. A mother of a soldier serving in Lebanon came into his office and started banging her head against the wall; she threatened suicide while pulling the hair out of her head and screaming that she wanted her son recalled from his combat unit in Lebanon. I suggested that her son be sent for immediately and that during the few days it would take for him to arrive, a non-combat solder should be assigned to visit her. In addition I suggested that she receive a letter stating that her son was on the way home. She should report back to Beno's office the following day at 11:00 a.m. promptly, and every day thereafter until the son actually arrived home. Somehow the mother was reassured by these steps. The son came on a brief visit... and the work went on in Beno's office.

And what work. Now he wanted me to concentrate on a particularly difficult set of problems. He wanted me to work with the staff whose job it was to tell parents that their sons had been killed. The only thing more difficult is to be on the receiving side of the evil tidings they are forced to bring. The people who perform this function are called, in the language of the street, "the Job's Patrol." "Do you tell them the bad news and then leave, or do you stay with them?" "How do you find people who can bear the strain of telling parents that their sons had been killed?" These are all reasonable questions amidst the insanity of war, questions which must be resolved.

These questions were shelved for the moment while I asked Beno if he could arrange a visit for me to the army jail. I told him the Timerman story and he contacted the officer in charge of the jail. In no time I had the paper with the necessary permission for the Timermans and myself to visit Danny in jail. They had visited him once already, and this was to be an "extra visit."

Next, I travelled to Tel Aviv to talk with Jacobo and Risha Timerman.

Should I go to the jail alone? Should Jacobo come with me? Should Risha? These were the questions we discussed as I thought to myself, can a man who has undergone torture in an Argentine jail withstand being in a jail where his son is interned? We discussed all these issues. At first, Jacobo wanted me to go alone. "You go, I know what it is like being in jail. Just seeing a friend of the family, a familiar face, when you are in jail is a big thing. You can talk to him about anything. Even the history of the fourth century and he will appreciate it. You go." In the end we decided that Jacobo would accompany me.

We met at 9:40 the following morning in front of the Atlit military prison. Atlit, where the crusaders had built a magnificent castle, where Jewish illegal refugees were imprisoned by the British, where plans were made to have the Yishuv's last stand during the Second World War if Rommel had succeeded in pushing beyond El Alemain and invaded Palestine, where Israel (to this day) has an army base, where the Arab prisoners of the Six Day War, the Yom Kippur War and now the Syrian prisoners of the Lebanese War are being kept. Here was Danny Timerman, son of Jacobo, kibbutznik, the archetypal Jewish prisoner of conscience. Danny, who didn't want to perform military police duties as a Jewish solder in Lebanon and was willing to serve a jail sentence rather than do it, was here.

If the weight of all those historical memories and the contemporary pain and absurdity weren't enough, in a few moments we were confronted with more.

The Sergeant Major greeted us at the gate. He took us up to the office of the prison's commanding officer, Major David. In his office there were five other officers and one civilian. They had obviously been in the midst of a discussion when we arrived. I knew every one of them from working together in the psychological unit of the army during the Yom Kippur and Lebanese wars. But I couldn't take my eyes off Yaffa, the only civilian and woman among them.

Yaffa is a dear friend. We had been through a lot together during the Yom Kippur War. She is permanently assigned to the psychological unit of the Israeli Army. I have worked with her since joining the unit more than ten years ago. Although a civilian, she is a central figure in the unit. She knows everything and everyone in the army. One can't do anything connected to the unit without her. She has lived through all of Israel's recent wars in the most intense way imaginable. Most of the brilliant officers, like Yonatan Natanyahu, of Entebbe fame, have been close friends of Yaffa's. Yaffa, although not more than forty, has seen more than her share of tragedies. For me, she *is* the Israeli army. Not only for me, but for many others I know.

Why?

Maybe it is because she was born in the Bergen Belsen concentration camp. Maybe because she is so very, very thin. Maybe it is because I feel the Israeli Army is protection for her. I don't know. But seeing her there in that room, at that time, with Jacobo present, was very difficult.

I introduced myself to the commanding officer, Major David, and presented Jacobo. David told me he was related to good friends of mine who had just visited Israel, and that his wife had studied with me at Haifa University. I turned to Jacobo, who had not followed all this since the exchanges were in Hebrew. I was about to explain, "we are among friends." But I couldn't form the words in my mouth. There was nothing to say to a father whose son is in jail. Nothing to say, that is, until he has seen and talked with his son. David said that he had placed a room at our disposal and that Danny would be brought to us soon.

We found the room where we were to meet with Danny. Two young army girls were there filling out some forms that looked like call up orders for soldiers to report to their units. There were no chairs in the room aside from the ones they were sitting on. One of them rose and offered to get some for us. My offer to help carry them was turned down and shortly the necessary chairs were arranged.

Then we waited for thirty minutes while music blared from the transistor radio that accompanied the preparation of the forms. There was occasional laughter and periodic visits by soldiers who evidently had designs on the girls. The drab, loveless atmosphere of the army environment was compounded by the fenced in feeling that only jails can produce.

Jacobo said, "Even though they knew that we were coming yesterday, it is only now that they are letting him take a shower and change clothes, it is like that in *all* jails."

Danny entered. He is a very special looking guy. Dark. Friendly. Alert. Vulnerable. Responsive. The softness of his exterior only brought into relief the toughness of the resolve he had demonstrated by defying the entire military system in Israel with his decision not to continue serving in Lebanon. I liked him the first time we had met at our home in Haifa. Marshall Meyer, the Argentine Rabbi well known for his human rights activity and other achievements had brought Danny and his family together with Jacobo and Risha Timerman to meet us. I liked him even more the second time when we met in Jacobo and Risha's apartment in Tel Aviv and had discussed his interest in cultural anthropology. But now there was something enormously heroic about him. Or at least my idea of heroism – quiet, unassuming, mundane, muted and a bit embarrassed by it all. I had seen precisely the same combination of qualities in Captain Zvika, the young man who had single-handedly destroyed sixty Syrian tanks during the first days of the Yom Kippur War.

But these were *my* reactions.

What was happening before my eyes was a very warm, loving and quite obviously mutually satisfying reunion of father and son.

Perhaps it was because my own father had died just a few months ago, or for a million other reasons, but the warmth of that reunion lit up everything for me. All I could think of was how right Anita had been to wake me up at 4:30. Bringing father and son together is an intrinsically valid act. In fact, helping to reunite families that are separated by any barrier is simply the right thing to do, whether those families are Palestinian Arabs or Russian Jews.

Even in the case of Israeli Jew Danny Timerman, the barriers between father and son had been extreme. The army required discipline. It was attempting to preserve social cohesion around a war policy which was tearing Israeli society apart. The requirement to continue his military duty in Lebanon was the one that helped create a physical barrier of concrete and barbed wire separating Danny from his family.

But there were other barriers, the kind that prevent reality from being apprehended directly, that filter understanding and prevent proper judgement. I wondered how strongly were they at work in this case, on both Jacobo and myself. Jacobo saw in every detail of the Atlit army jail reminders of the Argentinian jail in which he was tortured; I saw a regrettable but necessary system of restraint and control peopled by my friends, colleagues and students. Where Jacobo saw irredeemable and implacable evil, I saw an institution with severe doubts about itself and a willingness to adopt humane methods whenever possible. Jacobo was evidently intent on destroying the system and the mind-set that had imprisoned his son; I was inclined to search for ways to enable the people who managed it to show their humanity.

But what did Danny see?

He saw absurdity, stupidity, useless harassment. "They spend a lot of time here worrying about creases in blankets." While speaking to a fellow inmate sitting next to him during dinner, he had not heard an order to be quiet. He was then singled out and brought into a room where he was shouted at by a Sergeant and a girl soldier whose facial contortions were ugly, frenzied, and who appeared to be deranged. When Danny told them that they could shout as much as they wanted but the regulations forbade them from touching him, the Sergeant started to push him, just to demonstrate that indeed, he could. A fellow prisoner, a reservist who was a forty-five year old artist and holocaust survivor overheard the altercation and started to cry. The Sergeant had blond hair, and the Nazis had blond hair. They had shouted at prisoners like that and now...

I thought to myself that it was almost a logical, poetic necessity for there to be a Jewish Nazi-like incident associated with the internment of Danny Timerman. Several days before, upon release from prison, the artist had called the Timermans and told them about the incident. Jacobo had conveyed the details to me before our visit with Danny. But here it was. Danny was telling us directly about what had happened to him.

It was like so many other things one experiences in Israel. There is a kind of melodramatic necessity in the tragic and sometimes outrageous course of events. What would be rejected by a theater goer or a novel reader as cheap and manufactured is reality in this place. How absolutely incredible. Life in Israel becomes a permanent experience of *déja vu*, haunted by the past. Here in Israel, one can become the Golem that saves the Jewish people, but the Golem that destroys them as well. Not only is there the ever present possibility of destruction by enemies, there is also the possibility of becoming one's own worst enemy by adopting enemy tactics and directing them against the collective self. Even when this is not true in reality, the Jews in Israel constantly face the distorted accusations that they have adopted their oppressors' worst characteristics. And who are the most galling accusers? Fellow Jews.

Certainly, irrefutable proof exists that Jews can oppress themselves and others for whom they have moral responsibility. This is measure for measure run amok, where historical precedent becomes the script for contemporary enactments, where the future *is* the past with diabolic inversions and twistings. This, more than anything else, captures the reality of the Israeli experience and the challenge for the Jewish people.

We resolved with Danny to fight the system that could permit such brutal, inhumane embarrassment. But where? How? Jacobo talked of an international commission of lawyers, a possible suit against the Sergeant who had mistreated Danny. He gave his son a copy of the *HaOlam Hazeh* magazine containing pictures of Risha and of Danny's son at the huge Tel-Aviv protest to ensure an inquiry into the Sabra and Shatilla atrocity. We had all attended.

I gave Danny my gift of Plato's *Crito* and *Phaedo,* and he left to do his "work." We all said to one another that there were only ten more days until his release, but Jacobo said to me, "Do you have any idea what a day is to a person in jail?"

Standing outside, we discussed our next move. I suggested it would be wise to confront the officer in charge of this prison directly, to tell him of our outrage before we spoke to the General in charge of all army personnel. Jacobo agreed. We went to his office, sat down and waited. We helped ourselves to some sandwiches left on the table from the previous meeting, and shortly some hot coffee was brought in. Sitting there in the prison warden's office Jacobo reminisced about his prison experiences and about each of his three impressive sons. Hector is studying Political Science at Columbia University, George is also studying at Columbia, and Danny.

I mentioned that all in all the experience of standing up for one's beliefs and taking the consequences for one's actions must be a positive experience in a person's life. Danny would be stronger for what he is going through. I recalled my own confrontation with Sheriff Jim Clark in Selma, Alabama in 1964.

The discussion always came back to the question of what direction the Timerman family would take. Would they remain in Israel? There were divided counsels in the family on this point and the future was not clear. There seemed no doubt about Jacobo's Zionist commitment. However now he had finished two books, one on the Argentinian imprisonment and one on Israel, it was time for him to go on to other projects. Barbara Tuchman had considered Jacobo's latest book a "vile piece," while the editors of The New York Review of Book thought it very good. "What a storm it is creating."

After the second cup of coffee, David, the Officer in charge came in. He could not speak English well, and I translated for Jacobo what he had to say. I explained the set of circumstances surrounding our visit, and about the particular sensitivities of a father who himself had been tortured in jail. David said he had read Jacobo's book and had been moved by it. He was well aware of the special sensitivities. Furthermore, his parents had been in Auschwitz and he knew the scars such places can leave. His own parents had shared their feelings with him, and he could never forget.

He wanted Jacobo to know that he could not express his own political preferences while he was in uniform, but that he respected Danny's convictions. They had had a number of talks together which he enjoyed. He assured us that he had done everything permitted him to make the internment as bearable as possible. Danny was assigned work outside the prison for two days, was allowed to tend to some army business without guards outside the prison walls, and above all was not assigned to work units sent up to Lebanon – in order not to violate his convictions.

Danny's jail sentence was based on the assumption that men in uniform must "obey orders" for social order to be preserved. Without obedience to orders the law of the jungle takes over. It was not clear whether David was advocating the principle of obedience as an ultimate moral principle. Jacobo responded by questioning the moral principle implied, and it wasn't long before the discussion included the Greek insistence on a distinction between law and justice, and the prophet Amos' denunciation of immoral legalism... and of course, the

Nazi veneration of obedience above all other virtues was cited. David insisted that he was describing a mind-set rather than advocating it, and that when we had an opportunity to meet him out of uniform he would be glad to discuss the views he advocates. I wondered if we would ever meet him out of uniform.

Jacobo alluded to the Sergeant's harassment of his son. Evidently David had heard about it. He never apologized for it, but made it very clear that he had a serious problem. The role of the prison guard has a very powerful influence on the individual who has to fulfill its requirements. David cited research done with a group of normal University students in the United States. They had been randomly divided into "prison guards" and "prisoners," and were asked to play out their roles over a period of a few days. The identification with the respective roles was so great that there were acts of excessive punishment and cruelty.

He explained that the psychologists were here when we came into his office in the morning in order to discuss ways of innoculating ordinary soldiers who have to be prison guards against the morally debilitating effects of the role. The group had discussed an improved educational program for designated guards which included a redefinition of their function. I thought to myself that two thousand years of persecution in the Diaspora was apparently not sufficient training for the terrible roles which Jews have to assume in their own sovereign state. What about my two sons in their reserve army units? Would the situation every change and enable us freely to express the humanistic side of the Jew in Israel? As long as our enemies are determined to destroy us it is hard to imagine this happening.

Did Danny Timerman know that through his refusal to serve in Lebanon and to assume the policeman role he was perhaps forcing another Jewish boy to be brutalized through his role as guard in the prison where he was interned? Is there any possible moral inoculation against roles that are intrinsically morally corrupting? Is it better to be a *luftmensch* from Minsk or Pinsk who is sent to the gas chambers than to be the jailor of Danny Timerman? Is Atlit the inexorable outcome of Auschwitz, of Zionism, of a Jewish State, of the desire to remain alive as Jews? I think yes, and in my view, all we can do is to try to humanize the institutions we require in order to remain alive. It is the actual doing of it which is so difficult!

David continued, "Here you can read anything you want; the prisoners sleep outside in tents, not behind bars, in conditions frequently better than the field conditions of their regular units. There are visits from family and friends, and we are not very strict about the number of visitors." Jacobo interrupted. "In our family we have a skin problem which is hereditary. There is a pigment missing and we need special kinds of soap. I was told by the Chief Officer in Tel Aviv that I could not bring special soap to Danny, but it appears that I could have brought some. Why doesn't anyone know the regulations?"

Soap, skin, pigment. My fantasy was working overtime. We are talking about soap, skin and pigment in a Jewish jail, and everything is on the manifest level. All the latent associations, the historical memories were screaming at me, and it was all I could do to maintain self control. Both Jacobo and David were there on the level of realism. "Is it or is it not permitted to bring special soap into the prison if the prisoner has a skin problem?" David responded "Of course it is permitted!" That seemed to settle things for the moment.

Jacobo continued. "There is no provision for families in your procedures. No one from the army contacted us that Danny was in jail. No one told us what our rights are." David took out a soldier's file at random and showed us that the prisoners are asked whether they have notified their families that they are in jail. There it was in black and white. The prison had a form that asked whether family had been notified. David said that there were many prisoners who did not want their families to know they had been sentenced to an army jail. Since the maximum sentence in Atlit as twenty-eight days it was possible to keep the families from finding out about the sentencing. On the other hand, there are some soldiers who see their imprisonment for insubordination as a mark of bravado. "We have to be a bit careful about families and leave the decision up to the individual soldier."

"On visitors' day, why do you keep the parents waiting in a hot shed with only a corrugated roof, and where no smoking is permitted?" David was stumped on this one and remained quiet. "And finally, why don't your allow parents to bring food? This is the ultimate hardship on the visiting families. Even in Argentina families were permitted to bring prisoners food."

David explained that letting families bring food would introduce a lack of equality in the provisions prisoners received, and he could not allow that. Jacobo was unconvinced. In Argentina families were allowed to invite other prisoners who did not get food to share the food they brought. There is no question that Jacobo is correct, but it goes deeply against the Israeli mind-set. I could see before me the picture of children going to school in Israel. Over a million children go to school each day in jeans and the blue, white, or yellow shirt "uniform" of their school so that no children will feel deprived because their parents could not outfit them in the latest fashion. From age two or three until age twenty-one, most children in Israel are dressed in clothing similar to their peers for the same reason. The pressure for group norms and standardization is very great.

"In the prison, everyone gets the same food," David said.

We spent two hours in David's office. Two hours of discussion that ranged from abstract principles of justice, to historical lessons from centuries of Jewish history, to the mundane aggravations of imprisonment, to the parallels of life experience taken from Jacobo's imprisonment and torture.

We left David's office exhausted. We had come to destroy the system, and stayed to talk. Nothing much concrete was accomplished. David said to me as I thanked him for meeting with us that hardly a day goes by without a discussion like the one we just had. I said to him "Good."

On reaching the fresh air I said to Jacobo "Prisons are terrible places," and he answered "Yes, I know."

When I asked him if he wanted me to make an appointment with the General in charge of Human Resources in the army so that our protests could be heard on a higher level, he said he did not think that was necessary. "We have accomplished one thing. Now at least I know they will leave Danny alone, and that is all I want. No special favors, just left alone. Besides, he will be out a week from Friday." "In time for Shabat," I said. Jacobo shook his head.

We walked out to our waiting cars – he to return to Tel Aviv where Risha waited to hear every word of the meeting with Danny, and me to Haifa to share with Anita the results of the meeting she had shaken me out of my dreams to arrange.

Nothing much changed as a result of my intervention. Danny's sentence was not shortened. Jacobo's violent aversion to incarceration of any sort was not diminished one iota. The Israeli prison authorities were not further sensitized to human needs.

But a father had been reunited for a few short moments with a son who was sharing his father's fate in another, less virulent context, over different issues.

A former prisoner had re-experienced the trauma of confinement and torture in what was supposed to be an environment which would put an end forever to those things.

And all the rest of us, Anita, Risha, David, Yafe, the misguided and maybe demented Sergeant and his female accomplice, not to mention Danny and his wife and child, all of us, participate in the melodramatic reality that is everyday life in Israel. We continuously prove and reprove the banality of good and evil. I came out of the whole episode feeling that as long as we have in Israel the Dannys and the Davids we are all right. Maybe wishful thinking, but we shall see!

I got home famished and was very grateful that one of the avocadoes was soft enough to have for lunch. I love the Israeli variety, especially with lemon.

D. Passive Resistance – Full Circle: On The Wrong Side of Civil Disobedience

It is September, 1986. At the Cape Cod residence of Robert and B.J. Lifton, in their spacious cabin library, the annual meeting of the Psycho-History Association is taking place. Jean Elshtain has just made a first-rate presentation of her new book about women and war. Gene Sharp, the Director of the Non-Violent Alternatives to War Institute at Harvard passes me a note. "I would like to talk with you about a possible visit to Israel." Gene has written a number of books about non-violent alternatives to war. He asks me at the coffee break how I think the Israeli military would respond to his work on the subject of non-violent alternatives.

As the world now knows, Israel has developed a powerful military force. I could not imagine any group within the Israeli military taking an interest in developing non-violent alternatives to the Israeli-Arab conflict. So my immediate response was not what Gene expected. I said the Israeli military would probably be very interested in his work in order to plan more effective measures to counter non-violent strategies of resistance if they were ever adopted by the Arabs. Would it bother him if this was the approach to his work?

In response, Gene indicated that he was working with a number of Palestinians and had scheduled a trip to Jordan in the coming months. He would like to be exposed to the thinking of some individuals connected with the Israeli military.

A few weeks later, he called from Boston to arrange a meeting. I am far from being a spokesman for the Israel military, but I do happen to be connected with the Israel Institute for Military Studies directed by Dr. Reuven Gal, a former Colonel in the Israel Defense Forces and former Head of the Army Psychological Unit. The Institute is engaged in research on psychological issues relating to morale, decision making under stress, and moral behavior in combat conditions. Associated with the Institute are former high ranking army officers engaged in psychological research. Some of them are still serving in the reserves. I decided to arrange a day-long workshop with them around Gene's work on non-violent alternatives.

At 7:00 a.m. on the appointed day, I picked up Gene at his hotel in East Jerusalem. On the hour and a half trip to Zichron Yaakov, I told him about the individuals he was to meet with during the day.

When we arrived, we found all Gene's major works on non-violent alternatives to war on the conference table. Seated around the table were five of the most sophisticated Israeli social scientists, people holding doctorates from leading universities in the States and Israel.

Gene began by indicating that he has found himself in a difficult position of late. He has always supported Israel and does not accept the hardline PLO position that Israel has no legitimacy. However, he has been more and more troubled by the occupation of the West Bank by the Israeli military. Lately, he has become advisor to a group of Palestinians planning to use non-violent resistance in the Arab-Israel dispute.

He outlined for our group the various strategies analyzed in depth in his books. In addition, he described a number of apparent abuses of human rights perpetrated by Israeli soldiers on Arabs in the occupied territories. He found these incidents shocking because they did not appear consistent with the image he had of the morally sensitive Jew, conscious of the suffering of others. He could not understand how Jews could become oppressors.

The discussion during the day focused on two thing. First, the moral debilitation suffered by Israel's young army recruits when they are forced to maintain law and order during times of political unrest and revolt. We all agreed that in the long run, this undermined army morale and effectiveness. Second, would the Arabs have the capacity to generate a disciplined non-violent revolt against Israeli rule over the territories? We considered that Arab cultural and religious conditioning was not in tune with non-violent protest. It seemed impossible to imagine the Arabs engaging in the kind of non-violent resistance made famous by Gandhi and King. Gene Sharp, however, remained convinced that the Arabs could be mobilized to non-violent alternatives. My Israeli colleagues were left with an uneasy feeling that some American academics were passionately interested in fomenting non-violent confrontation.

Several weeks later an interview in the Israeli press indicated that Mubarak Awad had established an Institute in Jerusalem to encourage non-violent resistance to Israeli occupation. Awad makes no bones about his interest in applying some of Gene Sharp's techniques to the Arab-Israel conflict. It is too soon to assess his following, but he was recently joined by Hanna Seniora, who advocated a boycott of Israeli products (first cigarettes) in an attempt to have a financial impact on the Israeli occupation. Efforts to deport Awad from the country have to date been frustrated by a combination of support for him from Israelis and intervention from the American Embassy.

The throwing of rocks and molotov cocktails at Israeli army units is not the classic behavior of passive resistance. However, some of the actions of Arab schoolgirls and women against Israeli soldiers do have the mark of Gandhi and King.

How did we Israelis manage to become Goliath when just yesterday we were still the brave young Davids? Jewish history has been one of endless victimization. The Zionist Movement rejected passivity as a response to victimization and was instead determined to assume a mastery over its own fate in the ancient homeland. The horrors of Hitler's crematoria which killed six million Jews solidified the determination of those who survived never to let such a catastrophe recur. So against immense odds, the newborn State of Israel held its own against the armies of six neighboring Arab States which attacked following United Nations recognition. Those were heroic years.

Today, five-and-a-half years after our invasion into Lebanon, we find ourselves facing the determined resistance of a civilian population. The Palestinian refugees who fled their homes in 1948 have become the tragic victims of our determination to hold on to what we have gained. Each side feels itself the "true victim" and demands that the other side recognize its legitimate grievances and claims. We, the victim, have become the cruel oppressor. The sons, husbands, brothers and fathers of every home in Israel must spend time on the West Bank and in Gaza rounding up "unarmed" children who have hatred in their eyes and sharp stones in their hands.

Our country is deeply split politically. There are those who believe that only a strong hand will be respected, and that any sign of flexibility on our part will be interpreted as weakness to be abused and exploited. Others believe that the time has long been ripe to recognize the rights of the Palestinians to a state of their own and to mastery over their own destiny. And as this is being written, we have a Prime Minister who believes that one can resolve this tragic situation by pretending it does not exist.

Our neighbor's son was reading a book about the awful conditions in the Balaata Refugee Camp on the West Bank before he was drafted. His army unit was taken out of its basic training course and sent to the Balaata Camp during the first weeks of the West Bank disturbances. When he came home on furlough for the weekend, he found the book and put it away in a closet. "I can't read that now if I want to stay alive." That is what is happening. In our present untenable situation, we cannot afford to be humane because we fear for our lives. And yet, by not being humane, we are losing one of the most important aspects of our heritage.

Where does this leave those of us who have seen the majesty of Martin Luther King's resistance to white authority, but then have witnessed the degeneration of the Southern Christian Leadership Conference into violent Black Power, anti-Semitic "Harlem on My Mind," and Jesse Jackson?

If a choice must be made between dying as humanists or living as cruel masters, it is clear that we will choose to live. We have done our share of dying these many years. But for those of us who have experienced the passive resistance of a righteous cause, it is not at all clear that these are the only two alternatives. With the present strength and determination of the Israeli army, surely we can afford to take a chance and to be flexible.

The conclusion of all of this would seem to be that for us, at any rate, it is no sport to be hoisted with one's own petard.

Chapter Three

Retaining Identity Against the Fear of Death

Death in Israeli society is not associated only with wars, terrorism, heroic resistance and non-violent confrontation. As in all human societies, people in Israel live their daily lives with family and friends, and each individual confronts the reality of death within the context of her or her own life.

Our fear of death can paralyze our capacity to function. Overcoming such fear can be a major life work. The essays which follow describe how two individuals from very different life contexts confronted their death fears and overcame them.

Essay number one, *The Survivor as an Israeli Psychologist*, was written in 1980 within the context of a workshop on the Sociology of Psychology. The psychologist described was interviewed by a class in the attempt to discover the biographical framework of her psychological approach. Her death fears are a tragic part of the recent history of the Jewish people.

The second essay, *The Aborted Sibling Factor* (1983), is about a child who has experienced a different set of death fears. The context of her fears was neither specifically Jewish nor Israeli. She was a young Israeli child, and was helped to overcome her terrors through therapy provided by one of the authors as part of the Israeli support system.

A. The Survivor as an Israeli Psychologist

She walks in freshness. clean. The protective shield which filters out dankness, mildew, all the unwanted, has a glow to it. There is a vitality and liveliness to the whole ensemble. She is an athletic female of fifty or so, relishing the last vestiges of youthfulness. There is an engaging sweep to her entrances and exits. Her severely cut straight hair she wears like a comely hat – something like a Prince Valiant. She is not a lady you meet; you encounter her. Her eyes don't just look; they meet you and hold.

It does not take too long to find out that she was a young "maidchen" in Bergen Belsen concentration camp.

There her education started in earnest. As she puts it, "The beginning of my education, my realization of what the world is like, started in the concentration camp selection process." She distills in a few words the central lesson learned there: "I stood up to them, and lived." How, when, where are shrouded. But of one thing there is no doubt. She did something that worked – for her. And she is more than willing to share it with her patients.

She views the period before the Nazis as a kind of fairy-tale idyll. The small European town of her childhood was innocence itself. But uniquely so. Her birthplace, in her recollection, is distinguished first of all by what it was not. It was not an Eastern, nor a Western European country. It was not Slavic or Anglo-Saxon. It was something else. That something else has to do with the classical periods of Greece and Rome. The assimilated background she comes from means having been a fierce patriot, *not* speaking Yiddish, celebrating the holidays of many religions, not only one's own, luxuriating in the free and easy social intercourse between Jew and non Jew. School was infused with sports. A never ceasing integration of body and mind. It was the right proportion that counted. Balance and beauty. The whole thing was magnificent in her telling of it. But terribly naive, as she now judges it, and of course, gone forever.

Although her father served in the army, was a government administrator and owned property, although her mother was a talented pianist and studied in a Swiss music conservatory, still the Nazis came and destroyed it all. She was taken out of the Christian Monastery school where she had been studying and sent to the death camps. Her entire family was murdered. There is no one left beside herself.

As she recalls it today, the overriding quality of those around her at the time was their inability to believe in the possibility, not to mention the reality, of evil. Out of the seven thousand Jews in her town, only three left for Israel before the war. When speaking to them today, she asks them "Why didn't you tell us then – if you had a premonition of what was going to happen to us?" Their answer. No one would have believed them. And indeed, as she says now, they would not have. Her father, as transport administrator, had access to escape. But he stayed, and died, as did that whole world – for her.

Starting a new world, a new life, was not easy after liberation from the camp. There was some study and work in Budapest, in a large city instead of in the familiar town. There was a career to pursue; she settled for psychology instead of medicine. There was a marriage, an unhappy one, not what it should have been. And there was no way of making peace with the country people after what had happened. So, although she had to separate herself from a newly born child to escape, she left. She somehow got to Italy. Using false papers she managed to get her children out through the Joint. After some very difficult times indeed, she and her children finally joined her husband in Israel in 1950.

Israel was not easy either, but there was the joy and excitement of a fresh start. To this day she remembers with pride that she finished "first" in her Hebrew studies course. Like so many others with no Jewish education, no Zionist ideological background, and few Zionist convictions, she became an Israeli during a heroic period, the infancy of the new nation.

For the first few years she worked with immigrant children in Youth Aliyah, the organization set up to provide an educational framework for youthful refugees. Then, in 1958, she went to Europe to complete her doctoral studies. Her marriage did not survive the three year separation.

In Europe she was exposed to Binswangian Existential Psychology and to learning theory. She had some experience with Jungian theory and subsequently underwent an orthodox Freudian analysis. Her thesis managed to span the body-mind dilemma which had interested her since childhood.

When she describes her work one senses her strong humanistic conviction. She deplores conceptual rigidity of any sort. She is interested in "repair," a psychic repair which is achieved through "personal human contact." After she has ascertained the nature of a problem, her primary interest is to create this "warm personal contact." By creating greater self confidence in the patient, she believes, he or she can "open up." It is this personal human contact between therapist and patient which provides the "corrective experience and personal example," and these bring about helpful change in time.

Central to her view of the therapeutic role is an experience she had while training in Europe. "I was working in a Sanitorium. It was a kind of international home for wealthy, sick people. There were many ex-Nazi patients. When they learned of my Israeli-Jewish background, they became particularly frightened. The fear was that I was an Israeli secret agent – like the one that captured Eichman. In time they became reassured that I really wanted to help them. Treatment in that Sanatorium was not confined to specific hours, it was around the clock. I worked with those ex-Nazis very intensively. I even ate with them. I discussed their Nazi past with them at great length. I even treated patients who had been S.S. officers. They always tried to justify themselves to me, but I always told them my opinions. All of this was put to the test one day when one of the patients, an S.S. officer, invited me to go to the theatre. I agreed. Needless to say, my own motives were very complex, but they were fundamentally based on a desire to build a human bridge over the pain. I believe very strongly in creating a personal relationship.

When she speaks of these events one senses not only a powerful emotional experience, but an entire worldview encapsulated. She will never forget what happened – "How can I" But she is not able to hate the former Nazis. One has to hate the education they received, that they believed in. As for all those people who make an outcry against making peace with former Nazis, "What have they themselves done to relieve the suffering in the world?"

A strong social component informs her view about therapy. She feels that Jews in Israel have "brought many of the negative qualities they had in the Diaspora with them to Israel." It is mainly through corrective experiences like the ones she has with her patients that these negative qualities can be changed.

She declares that as a therapist she is prepared to accept the aggression, anger, guilt and frustration of the patient. But her role is by no means passive. "My therapy is directional. It is not a matter of spoiling, flattering and complimenting the patient. It often leads to confrontation."

Confrontation indeed?

It comes as no surprise to learn that she served for many years as the chief psychological consultant to one of Israel's elite commando units. One is struck by how the men in this unit share her qualities. Her eclecticism, suffering, triumphant assertiveness, physicality and raw courage bordering on adventurism all are there in so many of them. She offers her patients a model of the capacity of the self to prevail. It is the ascendency of her own "I" which communicates itself. The sheer boldness of it all.

Her boldness makes waves out in the society of which it is a part. While her announced purpose may be to repair and to provide corrective experience for individual patients, the effects of her work extend into society at large. Each of her many patients is slotted into a social role and has institutional connections. those who go through therapy with her come out of it fighting differently, loving differently, doing business differently. There is no way to keep the powerful energy she communicates contained within the individual human psyche.

She reflects her background by advocating parts of it and repudiating others. She advocates values she has come to treasure because they work for her. To deny them is to confront her – and she is ready for that possibility. But anyone who can say that clinical psychological practice is not a socially relevant enterprise, with social determinants and an intrinsic ideological stance towards the world, just has not met her.

B. A Child's Panic – The Aborted Sibling Factor

The number of abortions in the world is steadily increasing, and there are now millions of children whose mother aborted a sibling. This is not a subject which is often discussed, but there is increasing evidence that even very young children may be aware of maternal abortions despite family attempts to maintain secrecy. For some of these children the abortion of a sibling may be experienced as a mysterious death, and may trigger a serious reaction.

A child's death may be assumed to have a potentially traumatic impact on family members, and a sibling's death may continue to evoke fear, mourning and guilt in the surviving children if left unresolved. Three clinically typical adaptations to sibling death have been identified in family interactions. Krell and Rabkin (1979) speak of the "bound" child, who becomes overprotected and "precious," the "resurrected" child, whose existence is used to restore the missing sibling, and finally the "haunted" child, who must live with the secrecy and the fearful mystery surrounding the sibling's death. Our thesis is that a similar pattern may develop as a reaction to an abortion. The first two patterns may be typical in the case of a miscarried sibling. The element of secrecy around an abortion (in most families), arising from the parents' reluctance to burden their children with such a fact, may make the pattern of distrust and fear typical of the "haunted" child more prevalent in this case.

Awareness of abortion's impact on surviving siblings is new in professional literature (Cavenar, Spauling & Sullivan, 1979; Ney, 1983). But the few articles published confirm the thesis that children, even very young ones, may be aware of their mother's abortion although they are not told directly. As with all dramatic events, however, the child would have to be experiencing other powerful, unresolved conflicts which would then cathect to the trauma of abortion and to subsequent family dynamics before it became "haunted." We shall speculate on some of these other possible contributing circumstances in our final summary.

In this case, we therapists remained ignorant of the mother's multiple abortions for a long time. Even after hearing about them, we did not immediately connect them to the child's symptoms. Only the severity of the child's reactive fantasies to an abortion that had just taken place forced us to make the connection. And it was the child's dramatic recovery after superficial working through of the connection that confirmed its existence.

Case Study

Through a year and a half, various Community Services in the northern part of Israel joined to treat a sad, unassertive five year old girl. When she was first referred by the Family Health Clinic to her home area services, Laila was four years and two weeks old. She spent her time in the nursery school sucking her thumb and pulling her hair. She did not join in the activities of her companions; she seemed closed within herself. Her nursery school teacher was concerned with the extent of Laila's withdrawal, and was actively cooperating with the public health nurse in efforts to help her.

When Laila was first referred to the school psychological services (The Child Development Clinic), the nurse reported that she was fourth in a family of five children, and that she had been delivered through caesarian section. She was a large infant, weighing eleven pounds at birth, and had developed normally during her first year. By age two she was toilet trained, and she had no major illnesses over the years.

Three months after the original referral, Laila's mother at last agreed to bring her daughter to the Child Development Clinic for psychological testing. More information was gathered about Laila and her family.

Both of Laila's parents are from large Sephardi (North African) Jewish families, and both have only an elementary school education. They were married when Mrs. A was nineteen and Mr. A twenty-three, and all five children were born within six years. The father had been working steadily at his factory job since before the marriage; the mother never worked outside the home. The family, however, was known to the local welfare office because there were reports of frequent fighting between the parents. They were considering divorce – the mother complained about sexual incompatibility between herself and her husband.

Meanwhile, the children came to school showing evidence of neglect. Laila at age three, appeared to be dressing herself each morning, for she came with unmatched socks, and clothes inappropriate for the season. The brother, a year older than Laila, remained in kindergarten an extra year because he lacked appropriate stimulation at home. The Clinic also learned that the mother would occasionally disappear for a day or two without leaving adequate child care.

During psychological testing, Laila showed mainly normal capacity. She had no specific sensory-motoric difficulties. She was indeed extremely unsure of herself, but she responded positively to the supportive environment provided and to an individualized relationship. It was decided that her nursery school had too many children for such an insecure child, and that she would be transferred in two months, at the start of the new school year, to a special nursery school where she would receive more individual attention.

Laila's first few months in the new environment were spent sucking her thumb. She remained withdrawn into herself. She was completely unassertive and passively accepted the instructions of the teacher. She did however seem to enjoy the swing – her only assertive act was to ask the teacher for help if she had to get off.

A psychology student began working with Laila individually a few months after the school year began. Laila responded dramatically to the individual attention, and began to develop more self-confidence. After a few individual sessions, Laila mysteriously told the student that next week she would "be sick for a day" – but then she would come to see the student again. At the next session, she drew a flight of stairs and told about a child that fell down the stairs and died. She had a hard time leaving the student at the end of the session, and clung to her as long as possible. In the session after, Laila related every activity to death. First she said that someone killed the various objects she played with, and then she claimed that someone would come that night and kill her. She drew a man with a big nose, a fat man "like my father" that "swallows people." She said that she dreamed a snake came and ate her, but then corrected herself and said it was a lion.

A week later, she played aggressively with a doll, tearing off its head. She said it hurt the doll, but she continued to pull off whatever clothes remained on it and then said to it "that's that – now you can go away like that." During the session she looked for a gun "to kill with." Suddenly she looked at the student and asked her "why are you watching me?" It obviously bothered her. She was also unable to tell the student how old she was at that time.

In the student's summary of the five sessions she had with the child, she stated that Laila was an intelligent child with an ability to grasp things quickly. She had vast stores of energy untapped and closed off. She was easily accessible to an individual relationship, and told her thoughts openly, particularly through drawing.

The treatment sessions were important to Laila, and she was jealous that the student worked with another child as well. But unfortunately the student was unable to continue working with her.

However although the student's parting was hard on her, Laila had made significant gains in her behavior in the nursery during her weeks in individual treatment. Most of these gains remained with her. She was more cooperative with the other children, more physically active, and showed more self confidence. She still seemed preoccupied with her own inner world, but was more accessible to those around her.

Another psychology student worked with Laila a few weeks but the relationship was less intense. When Laila returned from the spring vacation she had regressed dramatically. She was more withdrawn and inaccessible than at the beginning of the year. Her thumb was almost never out of her mouth, and she lacked the energy to involve herself in any non-routine activity. It was recommended that she get individual treatment during the following school year.

Laila started regular kindergarten in September. The new kindergarten was right next door to her apartment house, for geographical proximity could help her to form relationships with neighborhood children. Then with the beginning of the school year, Laila began individual treatment with an experienced social worker who was being supervised in play therapy. Although Laila's behavior in the kindergarten was exactly like her original behavior in nursery school (thumb in mouth, completely withdrawn), her response within the context of the individual treatment was again dramatic. She did not suck her thumb during these sessions. Indeed, she made herself accessible to warmth and support. And though during the first session she required constant reassurance for self-chosen activities, from the second session on she walked, talked and played with more self assurance. But after about a month, when it seemed that the gains made during treatment might begin to be felt in kindergarten, there was suddenly another regression. Laila showed signs of real fear and withdrawal. She needed constant physical contact with the worker, but she also had a need to deny all feeing. "I am never mad, never not happy."

Throughout the previous year, the mother had been totally unresponsive and had come to only one of the four planned meetings. She had used that session to complain bitterly about her husband's sexual advances. So at this point we decided to reach out more to the parents and to visit the family at home. During the first visit the mother was out. The father was home however, and although all previous reports had described him in strongly negative terms, he was most willing to sit and talk about his children. He even expressed real concern for Laila and her "sensitivities." He claimed that only his oldest son and Laila were so "moody," and that the three other children were more mischievous.

In an effort to discover the root of Laila's two regressions since she had been in individual treatment, we discussed what life had been like for the family during the last year. It became apparent that each of the two regressions (during spring vacation, and only the week before) coincided exactly with the hospitalizations of Laila's older brother – the boy who had been linked to her emotional sensitivities by the father.

As a result, we made the hospitalization of Laila's brother the main theme in her subsequent therapy. She was totally enthralled, insisting on playing out her visit to her brother again and again. Furthermore, her behavior began to be somewhat more assertive. It seemed her problem might be rooted in overidentification with a sickly sibling – especially when in one of these sessions, she drew a picture of her brother on one side of the page, and then turned it over to trace herself on the exact opposite side! Moreover in all her drawings during the previous weeks she had produced rigid stick figures without ears and arms. At the end of the second "hospital" session, she added two arms and ears to the pictures of her brother and herself.

A second home visit followed. This time both mother and father were home. But Mrs. A seemed physically ill and reluctant to talk – until the worker happened to ask her if she was perhaps pregnant. With obvious gratitude Mrs. A began to express deep feelings of hopelessness and rage at the fact that she was once again pregnant. She did not want any more children; five were enough. Besides, she had begun to work in a nearby factory a few hours each day and she loved getting out of the house and meeting people. Her husband had finally consented to her working, but now everything would go back to being no good. In the discussion which followed, it became clear that Mrs. A had never used contraceptives, and that she had already had four abortions – the last six months before.

Both Laila and the fifth child (a son) had been delivered via Caesarian section. Consequently the Ministry of Health had granted her easy access to abortions. She assumed the only thing to do now was to have another abortion, and she had already made inquiries for next week. She claimed she was not medically allowed to use the I.U.D. She inquired hesitantly of the worker about the possibility of fallopian tube closure, and seemed willing to explore ;the possibility with her doctor if her husband agreed.

So Mr. A was invited into the room. He also felt five children were enough. And both agreed that so many unwanted pregnancies had caused great tension between them, since Mrs. A was in constant fear of another pregnancy. The obvious solution was that they go together to the Health Clinic and arrange for a tubal ligation.

When I arrived at Laila's kindergarten the following week, the child was in another state of regression. She spoke in a whisper, clung to me, and totally lacked self assurance. During the play session she spoke of the fact that her mother was away once again. She suggested that she herself had been in a terrible accident the day before, but there was no visible sign of this and it was not confirmed by the teacher. Most significantly, when the hospital game was played, and I asked Laila what a little girl could be so very afraid of, she at once answered "of her mother." And when I named the five family children, Laila said, no, her mother had eleven, not five children.

It was not until after this session that the pieces of the puzzle fell together. Evidently Laila was reacting to her mother's abortion the previous day (hence the "terrible accident"). By looking back once again at the record, we discovered that the mother's fourth abortion had occurred just when the first psychology student began to work with Laila – and Laila had spoken about children falling down stairs and had dreamed of being killed. Laila's spring and fall regressions had coincided with her brother's hospitalizations, and now she was experiencing with terror her mother's fifth abortion. When Laila spoke of her mother's having eleven children, she included the five abortions, and she may have included another Laila since her mother is a twin.

We hastily reviewed the early play sessions. Now, Laila's fear of being killed at night seemed related to her fear of her mother, a woman who could "kill" her own children (embryos). And when her brother was hospitalized, it seemed Laila considered it proof that his turn had come and perhaps hers was next. With such powerful fears of survival, no wonder she had withdrawn so dramatically.

We decided the issue needed to be confronted head-on, for all its painful delicacy. Laila was told in many ways that although an embryo is alive, it is not yet a person, whereas Laila herself and her brother are people, and her mother and father wanted them to be alive and well. I stressed that Laila was a little girl with lots of capabilities, and that all the people who knew her and loved her, like her parents, her teacher, and myself wanted her to do well and to be healthy. Her parents also wanted her brother to be well; that was why he had been treated in the hospital.

Laila listened with wide-eyed attention. She nodded solemnly a few times, particularly when I stressed how strong and capable I knew Laila was. But there was one cloudy point which she asked about: her father was fat; had he swallowed the babies? Would he give birth to them?

She had a need to hold on to this fantasy, and so did not absorb the objective information readily. But she did show a remarkable capacity to use the information given her. By the following week her kindergarten teacher was reporting that her behavior had changed dramatically. She had a greater ability to participate in group activities. And the change persisted through the following months.

Interestingly, during the week when the pieces of the puzzle began to fall together, I saw a drawing by a seven year old child who was also in treatment. The child had drawn a flower pot with seven flowers in it. Three of the flowers were drawn in full red colors; the other four were only outlined. The child was the second of three live children in a family where there had been two abortions, one stillbirth, and a child who died at age six months.

Discussion and Summary

In the case I have presented, a five year old's extreme regression gradually led to the suspicion that she was experiencing a severe reaction to her mother's multiple abortions. When this issue was raised and worked on in therapy, the child's dramatic recovery seemed to verify its significance. The existence of a plausible link between the mother's abortion and the sibling's reactive disorder requires us to speculate on the circumstances under which such serious reactions would be most likely to occur. Clearly, not all, nor even most siblings have such reactions.

Two factors seem central. First, the child's developmental stage when the mother has the abortion. Before the age of two it is doubtful that a child could conceptualize the death of a potential sibling whose presence has not yet been concretized through birth. And after age eight, most children can differentiate between the murderous thoughts which all children feel from their parents and planned aggressive action directed at another. Between three and five, children seem the most vulnerable to these distortions and misconceptions.

During these years, the child still feels the omnipotence of infancy and is subject to magical thinking. This is the age of Oedipal conflicts, when rage and jealousy experienced towards the parent of the same sex may easily be attributed to feelings of reciprocal rage and destructiveness. "I wish my mother (or father) was dead" can blend magically into "She (he) knows I wish her (him) dead so she (he) wants to kill me. She (he) is dangerous because she (he) can kill babies." We know that such distortions arise in a response to separation from parents at this age, and we may reasonably assume they exist around the "mysterious" issue of sibling abortion.

The second factor is the home atmosphere. All homes have periods of tension and anger, and all parents experience feelings of rage at their children. An unwanted pregnancy can certainly heighten feelings of frustration and resentment toward those children who are already draining the family's emotional and physical resources. In homes where these resources are particularly limited and where marital tensions interfere with feelings of mutual support, an unwanted pregnancy may arouse real hostility on the part of the mother or father toward their children. That hostility may be experienced by a child as truly "murderous." Where the potential for violence is experienced either through the active abuse of children or through passively hostile neglect, an abortion can be, for the preschooler, a proof of the parent's capacity to be dangerous. In middle class homes where the hostility may be more heavily veiled, an abortion and its surrounding mystery can be experienced as a concrete violent act.

These two factors are at present solely in the realm of speculation, since we know of no research attempted in this area. The subject is as yet largely unexplored in the professional literature. With the vast increase in abortions around the world over the past decade, however, we must investigate the potential consequences of such abortions on surviving siblings. It is our hope that the case presented may make the relationship between maternal abortion and potentially destructive sibling reactions known so that the linkage may be more immediately available to therapists working with children.

Chapter Four

Living With War and Death

In Israel the constant presence of war or the threat of war is nothing new and needs no elaboration. The four essays in this chapter were written over a period of seventeen years as perspective evolved.

They reflect both authors' growing knowledge of and experience with war-related death in Israel. "The Mutability of Youth: History From an Adult Perspective" was written in 1970 during our first year in Israel. It responded to the euphoric adulation of heroism following the Six-Day War. "Making the Dead Make the Living: The Dynamics of Heroization" (1972) resulted from research on the memorial rites for fallen soldiers during the long War of Attrition.

"Retrieving the Living: Israeli Reaction to Bereavement in War" was written in December 1973, after the shock of working with over forty bereaved families during the Yom Kippur War. The fourth essay, "Death: A Threat to War's Legitimacy" (1986) is the accumulation of many years of experience in the army reserve unit which deals with the families of fallen soldiers.

A. The Mutability of Youth: History From an Adult Perspective

The behavior of Israel's youth during the 1969 Six-Day War is widely considered exemplary. As warriors they were intrepid, and ultimately invincible. As humanitarian victors they were for the most part compassionate and philosophically reflective. And yet, adult criticism of Israel's youth before the Six-Day War was at times withering. How could Israeli adults have so misjudged the qualities and capacities of their youth? How could they have been so wrong?

Of course, there are a number of problems with the question. First, it assumes that evaluations by adults are objective statements about the condition of youth, that they are based on facts and correspond to reality. Second, it assumes the adults were wrong in their initial evaluation. Perhaps they were right. Being a "bad" young person during a period of relative peace may be just the right preparation for being "good" in a war situation. The question assumes, but does not prove, a contradiction. Third, the question's phrasing fails to consider that criticism of the young may be necessary for their socialization. Maybe the only way to make them "good" is to call them "bad."

We prefer to pose the question in different terms. What kinds of critical comments about youth were made in Israel by adults before the Six-Day War? And what, if any, was the impact of the young people's laudable war-time performance on these comments? By presenting the question this way, we stress that our first task is to examine the *statements* made by adults rather than the *condition* of the young before and after the war.

And the following supplementary questions apply: 1) Which specific characteristics of youth have the adults denigrated? 2) According to the adults, what causes these negative characteristics? 3) What remedies do they suggest? 4) What can we learn about the adults from the characteristics they choose to criticize in the young?

In order to answer our questions, we have analyzed statements taken from three Israeli morning newspapers both before and after the Six-Day War. We selected these three newspapers because they reflect the opinions of adults from three distinct population groups. *Davar* is the major organ of the labor movement, which controls a sizable portion of the state's political 'power' and economic resources. *Ha'aretz*, the most influential semi-independent paper, has a more academic readership. *Hatzopheh* is directed to the religious community. We used the standard methods of content analysis, which attempt to quantify the material systematically and objectively. We selected sentence fragments and words from articles evaluating the young that appeared in the three newspapers between 1965 and 1970.

We selected articles according to the following principles: 1) they must be written by adults; 2) they must be evaluational, containing praise or criticism of the behavior of the young. For our purposes we defined young people as those in their late teens or early twenties. We did not include in the sample articles on specific problems such as juvenile delinquency, reports of sociological or psychological research, interviews with young people, purely descriptive essays, or weekend supplement pieces, which have a character of their own. A total of one hundred and eighty articles met our criteria, and we chose forty-three of them for our sample.

We classified sentence fragments in the following manner: a) alleged negative characteristics; b) alleged positive characteristics; c) hypothesized causes of alleged negative characteristics;

d) recommended solutions; e) statements made before or after the Six-Day War; f) the type of newspaper.

Our results were as follows:

1. Before the war, 97 percent of *Davar*'s descriptive terms were negative, and only 3 percent positive.

2. A relatively high degree of criticism prevailed in all three papers, even in the euphoric period after the war. Fifty-one percent of the descriptive terms had negative implications despite the acknowledged laudable performance of the young in the Six-Day War and the War of Attrition which followed.

3. The *degree* of change in opinion after the war was relatively consistent for each paper (i.e. 46 percent, 38 percent and 45 percent).

4. *Hatzopheh*, the paper for the religious community, published more positive evaluations of the secular, non-religious young than did *Davar*.

Before the war, young people's shortcomings were considered noninvolvement and detachment. But from what? The three newspapers do not agree. In *Davar*'s case the young were detached from land and values; for *Ha'Aretz*, they lacked good ;citizenship and public responsibility; for *Hatzopheh*, they had become estranged from Jewish traditions. In a society requiring its youth to be involved in defense and settlement, detachment and disengagement are perhaps the most devastating charges that can be levelled.

Striking correlation occurs between the ownership and readership of each newspaper and the characteristics attributed to the young before the war. Each newspaper's evaluation reflected its own dominant values. For *Davar*, settlement of the land and guidance by labor ideology were the important *a priori* values. For *Ha'Aretz*, responsible, enlightened citizenship was essential. *Hatzopheh* held commitment to Jewish traditions as central. So while we cannot reconstruct or ascertain whether these newspapers were describing the true state of Israeli youth at the time, it is quite clear that they were saying a great deal about themselves in the process.

Social psychological literature has clear opinions on the issue of *a priori* judgements and their impact on descriptions. Most descriptions, even when they purport to be objective, are very far from being so. The Israeli press is just another case in point. What is curious is the apparent lack of self awareness on the part of these newspapers.

The consistency we found between the newspaper ownership's *a priori* values and their pre-war negative judgement of youth, appeared once again in their enumeration of positive characteristics after the war. The labor paper, *Davar*, perceived the young, now considered good, as spiritual, intellectually constructive, and idealistic. *Ha'Aretz* saw them as more conscious of their civic responsibilities and more politically minded, while *Hatzopheh* considered them open-minded and desirous of contact with tradition. This last is about the best compliment a religious person can pay to one who is not observant.

Evidently, the terms of reference after the war remain the same, but the evaluation has become positive. Now, the young are said to have the very same traits that each newspaper found lacking before the war. Apparently the need for internal consistency is so strong that it defies common sense. Rather than discover totally different positive attributes, and thus avoid the embarrassment of a wrong earlier assessment, the papers credit the young with precisely those qualities they previously lacked.

What did the young do during the war to cause such a change in the overall evaluation of their conduct? They behaved like good soldiers. No necessary link exists between fighting the good fight and participating in the "spiritual revival" attributed to the young. However, each of the three newspapers had an ideological filtering mechanism which picked out connecting links between good soldiering and the positive characteristics they discovered in the young. The common denominator between the three newspapers was their praise for *involvement*, but the kind of involvement praised was different for each. *Davar* praised spiritual and intellectual involvement, *Ha'Aretz* praised political and moral involvement, while *Hatzopheh* praised readiness for possible religious involvement.

Involvement as a characteristic was seen positively by all three newspapers, but that involvement was qualified by institutionally linked explanations which had a high degree of consistency. It is clear from our findings that the descriptive process adults engage in when writing for newspapers about Israel's youth is anything but neutral.

The data we collected in our study gave us many clues as to the structure of adult consciousness in Israel. We found the same threads running through the causes given for youth's behavior as we had found in the previous negative and positive evaluation of their behavior. *Ha'Aretz* found the cause in political and institutional factors; *Davar's* causes were spiritual and ideological; *Hatzopheh's* causes were religious.

For *Davar*, war and peace are the central factors influencing the behavior of youth. Unlike the other two newspapers, which do not even mention war as a factor, *Davar* gives the 1967 war a central position. Before 1967 comparative peace is given as the major reason for young people's negative behavior. After the war, *Davar* reads the tense security situation as a positive restraint for youthful rebelliousness. According to the point of view expressed in the labor daily, war builds up moral character.

But what of *Ha'Aretz* and *Hatzopheh?* In these two newspapers the war and the country's security were not even mentioned as factors in the behavior of youth. What then was the connecting link found in them between good fighting and either assuming more civic responsibility (*Ha'Aretz*) or becoming more religiously receptive (*Hatzopheh*)? Since the subject is not spelled out in these sources as it is in *Davar* we can only speculate.

We consider that although *Ha'Aretz* and *Hatzopheh* do not mention the positive moral impact of war, they nevertheless accept it as a fundamental premise – it does not seem possible that a labor minority could maintain its power for so long despite strong political opposition if it did not voice sentiments that the other parties shared but felt inhibited from expressing.

Interestingly, all three dailies agreed on adults as prime causal agents in the behavior of the young. All three assume that the young are unable freely to generate their own behavioral patterns, and they depict the young as acted upon rather than initiators of action. It thus follows that they cannot be blamed when they behave badly. It is the adults who must be held responsible.

The papers offer two basic solutions for handling youth's alleged negative characteristics. The first is a rather diffuse moral preaching: "Develop the value of humility in young people." The second specifies modes of implementation: "Co-opt young people into positions of leadership." All the solutions imply that the young are not capable of dealing with their own negative qualities and that it is the responsibility of adults to educate and guide them.

The remedies advocated by *Davar* and *Hatzopheh* before the war exhibit a curious combination of belief in abstract values and mass communication technology. *Davar* recommends the use of cinema and *Hatzopheh* recommends mass media to influence the behavior of the young. However after the war these two newspapers, which had earlier stressed the value of humility, now express appreciation for the individualism of the young, and advocate setting challenges for them. After the war the young are no longer to be controlled and disciplined.

In *Ha'Aretz* we found a distinction between the post-war period during the War of Attrition and the period following the cessation of hostilities. During the War of Attrition, *Ha'Aretz* stressed spiritual values and the content that should be provided to the young as the country looked ahead to a time of peace. After the 1970 ceasefire, the paper stressed the importance of "intellectual achievement rather than values alone."

Clearly newspapers easily accommodate themselves to the fact that their own evaluations have proven wrong and are able to shift ground without apparent misgiving.

In conclusion, when Israeli adults evaluate the young in newspaper articles there is no necessary correlation between their evaluation and the actual behavior of the young. We have not been able to demonstrate directly the absence of such a correlation, but we have presented some strong evidence to show that adult evaluations lack objective validity.

Further, a remarkable consistency exists between the evaluations made about the behavior of the young and the institutional situation of the adults doing the evaluating. This consistency is so great that once one knows the institutional affiliation of an adult who is evaluating youth's behavior, one can predict with a high degree of certainty how the youth will be described, the reasons ascribed to behavior, and the remedies advocated. It is possible that this predictability of adult responses may serve an important function in successful socialization. In the meantime, however, our data seems to show that when adults attempt to be objective in their description of the young, they are instead describing themselves and their own values.

B. Making the Dead Make the Living: The Dynamics of Heroization

Rituals surrounding death provide many clues to tribal values for anthropologists studying primitive peoples. Modern societies, too, reveal themselves in their responses to death. A trenchant sociological analysis of modern society's funeral rites may bring the observer as close as he can get to that society's innermost core of values. Most societies find it difficult to live with the oppressive reality of death. Israel is no exception. But Israel's rituals associated with death have some unique aspects. In this essay we will analyze these rituals in order better to understand the values of Israeli society.

The Jews in the Diaspora, outside of Israel, respond to death through elaborate ritual. They recognize grief publicly, refuse to deny the loss psychologically, engage in seven days of mourning and thirty days of abstinence from merrymaking, pray a special Kaddish prayer daily for eleven months, participate in yearly memorial services which they integrate into the Jewish holidays, and celebrate an annual memorial on the anniversary of the death. These institutionalized forms are relatively well known and some have their parallels in other religions. But what of the reaction to death once Jews live in a Jewish state? Are there any intrinsic differences or unnoticed particularities under the new condition? We think there are.

Most strikingly, in the Jewish State rituals much more frequently celebrate the heroic, bold, brave, gallant and valorous dead. Those deaths which are not heroic Israel shares with the Diaspora – those of the ordinary dead who are for the most part unseen and silent; the venerable and martyred dead; the pitiful dead. In this essay we will focus on the response to Israel's recently commemorated heroic dead.

Despite the veneration they receive, the heroic dead have much competition for attention. Jews have been dying in Israel for at least 4,000 years. The country overflows with reminders of other claims for priority, claims that are impossible to ignore. For example, the Mount of Olives in Jerusalem is a raw mountain with thousands of artless gravemarkers; in Bet Shearim in the Southern Galillee lies a vast, largely unexplored city of tombs from the period of the Mishna and the Talmud. Every year we discover more family sarcophagi, more burial caves.

Israel's ancient dead have a number of characteristics that set them apart. First and most salient, their ubiquity. A friend of mine found a large burial cave while building his home near Haifa; just recently a workman digging a ditch found one in Nablus. So the Ministry of Religion needs a group of busy men to go around collecting bones that have been unearthed and then giving them a respectful reburial.

Second, Israel's ancient dead are periodized, and thus historically relevant. Dried bones found in the stratigraphy of an archeological site, such as the layers of skulls and bones in Caesarea, offer indispensable indications of past civilizations. They enable definitive identification of the strata as Roman, Byzantine or Crusader. Indeed, entire sites have been assessed by the direction of a skull – whether it faced Jerusalem or not – or by a skeleton's crossed arms.

Third, Israel's ancient dead are politically powerful. They tend to substantiate Jewish claims to particular geographical areas. Every time a Jewish burial site is found in occupied territory it gives greater legitimacy to Israel's claims for the land in which it is found. The television announcer on the evening news might say; "At such a period this land was ours." While it is absurd to imply that every place where Jewish bones are to be found belongs to Israel, the gravesites offer an emotional connection to the land that adds greater legitimation to claims for it.

Fourth, Israel's ancient dead are venerable and sacred. When we find bones in excavations, we call not the Health Department but the Ministry of Religious Affairs. Old bones in Israel are not disposable litter; in accordance with Jewish Law they are religiously potent. They have the power to contaminate those with 'Cohanim,' priestly lineage. When bones surface during excavation for a new building, all construction must cease until the Ministry of Religious Affairs determines the circumstances surrounding them.Some of the more violent demonstrations in Jerusalem have arisen because a suspected cemetery has been discovered during construction or archeological excavation. Those who build or explore do not appreciate being hampered by the Religious Authorities. The religious in turn regard the indiscriminate disturbance of burial tombs as an unforgivable sacrilege. Ancient bones are thus frequently a source of modern headlines.

The last major characteristic of Israel's dead, and perhaps the most difficult to formulate, is that their bones are reminders of death as well as the fundament upon which the living walk. Somehow, in Israel, the dead are more alive. In any country one feels the peculiar pathos of the dead – their tragedy and finality but also their indispensability and potentiality. Here in Israel there is something more. Just like the dry bones in Ezekiel's vision, these bones are potentially alive. They can acquire living flesh in a trice and start to move. Israel's ancient dead are not simply the necessary condition to life today, they are potentially the sufficient conditions. They convey the message, as in rabbinic legends of resurrection, that even if no Jews remained alive one could create them with bones alone.

In brief, Israel's ancient dead are always potentially contemporary, and remain so with a special intensity. Resurrection remains an imminent possibility and, insofar as it does, all of Israel's dead are alive.

But what of Israel's contemporary heroic dead? Who are they? By "heroic" dead we mean people who have been honored after death with public praise for acts of distinguished valor and fortitude. If we consider those killed in Israel's six major wars – the War of Independence (1948), the Suez Campaign (1956), the Six-Day War (1967), the War of Attrition (1967-70), the Yom Kippur War (1973), the Lebanon War (1982) – there are thousands. The most recent figures? In the Six-Day War 777 soldiers were killed and 2,811 were wounded; during the War of Attrition 594 solders died, 959 were wounded; in the Yom Kippur War more than 3,000 lost their lives and more than three times that number were wounded; in the Lebanon War over 600 have died to date and thousands more have been hurt.

Thus, from the past seventeen years we have close to 5,000 candidates for the status of individualized hero. But despite the public rhetoric, which makes all Israel's war dead heroes, there is a difference between an individual hero, one who is known and treated with individualized rites, and one who is not. It is the process by which individuals are made into heroes that interests us.

Two major obstacles prevent every fallen soldier from becoming a hero. They are found not in the "true" circumstances of death but in its social context. What are these social conditions? First, perpetuating the individual memory of a dead hero costs. If the story of heroism is to endure – and that is the point of it – it must be concretized with a visual symbol. Heroism atrophies with time if it is not continuously celebrated. Emerson referred to this fact when he wrote: "Every hero becomes a bore at last." Keeping the heroic act fresh, memorable and interesting is a formidable enterprise. It requires imagination, tact and persistence.

Concretizing heroism requires forms that take money, time, materials and sometimes land. Thus, there are limits to how much individualization of heroism a society can permit itself. If every man's death is celebrated as heroic, the society can go bankrupt. Indeed, some primitive tribes periodically do just that because of the ruinous expense of funeral and memorial rites.

The second condition preventing the heroic coin from being devalued, preventing every man's death from being celebrated as heroic, is the pressure of the "haves," in this case the friends and family of already publicly acknowledged heroes. They are a natural pressure group that press for a sober, restrained distribution of accolades. In a society that is at war for many years, they need to remain in a constant state of alert. There are always the newly killed whose memorable acts and death are more manifestly relevant to the here and now.

An uneasy alliance of fate joins the families of the dead from different periods. There is an ongoing process of redefinition of the dead soldiers' venerability, and a constant re-evaluation of heroic periods. And emotions remain intense throughout the entire process. For while long-dead heroes who have been celebrated become more redoutable with age, the demands of the recent dead for recognition are most poignant and pressing. In Israel's National Organization of Bereaved Families, Yad LeBanim, all the factors mentioned are at work.

Two other factors have sedulously worked against the recognition of individual heroism in Israel; the equalitarian ethos and the spirit of voluntarism. These factors have not been sufficiently powerful to prevent the recognition of individual heroism, but they have impeded its development. First, a hero is not like everyone else; that is the point of giving him recognition. But in a society which aspires to equality, the self conscious creation of elites is regarded as counterproductive. Second, Israel's precarious position prior to the Six-Day War required a high degree of voluntarism from the average citizen. The extraordinary valorous and zealous act on behalf of the group was the norm rather than the ideal. Each person had to extend himself to the limit. It is particularly hard to single out individuals for special veneration in a situation such as that.

But in spite of the many obstacles some of the dead do become heroes. Yosef Trumpeldor was killed in the twenties, before there was a hero-creating institution, and was recognized as a hero. The recognition of his heroism was idiosyncratic and singular. Recently, Israeli heroism has become organized and institutionalized with state-sanctioned procedures, ceremonies and memorials that acknowledge, publicize and perpetuate. This is a new phenomenon.

Although the procedures were hesitantly instituted and ambivalently implemented, now they are an established part of the institution. Every Israeli schoolboy now knows that a "Tzalash" is a mark of commendation for military heroism.

The "Tzalash" was instituted at the insistence of Jewish soldiers trained in the British Army – despite objections from the Palmach, the original elite Jewish Defence Unit. Comparatively few "Tzalashim" are meted out. What course is open for those whose dead did not receive a "Tzalash"? Did their sons not die fighting? Are they not to be acknowledged, publicized and perpetuated as heroes? Of course. But how?

In Israel, relatives and friends of fallen soldiers can perpetuate the heroic memory of their dead in two ways: erecting a monument or writing a book. Each is interesting in its own right.

Consider the Red Rock of the Negev. On July 8, 1971, ten air force personnel died under mysterious circumstances. Their plane crashed offshore near a Bedouin encampment between Rafiah and El Arish – which was occupied territory following the Six-Day War. The soldiers' families decided to erect one memorial for all ten. But where? The parents were sure that the territory would remain under Israel's jurisdiction, so in an act of faith they decided the monument should be on the beach near the site of the disaster. Their attitude toward the occupied territories seems to be typical of bereaved parents: "Our boys have died for this land and it belongs to us."

What kind of memorial can one erect for ten young men? The parents decided it was to be something large but simple. A rock! But not any rock. They organized an expedition to search for a suitable one in the Sinai peninsula. Finally, after much searching, they found a rock near Mount Sinai. It measured thirty-five by thirteen by seven feet. Getting it to the site was a prodigious undertaking, but they managed. There on the beach, at the site where Yamit was yet to be built and later yet disbanded, they placed the rock from Sinai to commemorate the death of ten Israeli fliers.

When the rock was dedicated in the presence of 1,500 friends and relatives of the ten, Prime Minister Golda Meir said, "This monument perpetuates the memory of the ten; the elite among the warriors of Israel." In memorial ceremonies this note of apotheosis consistently re-echoes. The number ten with all of its potency – the ten commandments, the minyan (the basic unit for public prayer) – appears as a mystic, symbolic accompaniment to the act of commemoration. The most revealing words were uttered by the commanding officer of the Southern Region: "In their death, the ten join the long line of Israeli warriors who have given that which is most precious – the existence, security and peace of the land of Israel."

He continued, "The monument of the ten has become another of the cornerstones in the settlement of Israel's boundaries. I know that there is no consolation for bereaved parents but perhaps there is some consolation in this: that by their last deed the ten have transformed this desolate beach into a place bustling with life." Not surprisingly, the rock became a rallying point for those opposing withdrawal from the Sinai after the Camp David Accord. Forfeiting the Red Rock monument during the evacuation of Yamit was a public trauma for all concerned.

Here, then, are all the ingredients of heroism: potent symbols, important personages, unrestrained homage, a promise of life to overcome desolation. We have chosen only one of the memorials erected, but the same could be written about the thousands to be found all over the country. Not all are rocks. Some are burned out tanks, others huge concrete structures or metal masses, or curtains to cover the Ark of the Torah in the Synagogue, or rooms set aside at Kibbutzim, or large buildings devoted to the memorabilia of the fallen heroes. All these empty cenotaphs share as the primary function the purpose of acknowledging, publicizing and perpetuating heroes.

Shelley's poem "The Cloud" treats the cenotaph lightly. "I silently laugh at my own cenotaph and arise and unbuild it again," he wrote. But in Israel cenotaphs are serious affairs. They are built to last. Maybe in some future day there will be silent laughter, but it is still not around. Some avant-garde writers such as Hanoch Levin and Sara

Chinski dare to question the reverence, but their attempts are not widely accepted. The sorrowful memories are too fresh for that.

It is unlikely that true peace will come to the Middle East until all the cenotaphs in all the countries in the area are unbuilt. That will take some doing. In the meantime we may have to settle for a more realistic perception of death, with the hope of restraining aggression. Golda Meir remarked that peace may come to the Middle East when all the countries' chiefs of state leave standing instructions with their war ministers, as she did, to wake them at night every time someone is killed in any hostilities. Her point? Every country *honors* its war dead. The important point is to value the living.

Israeli-Jews perpetuate war heroes through a different kind of monument too – the memorial book.

I first became interested in Israel's literature of the war dead when a relative gave me a book as a welcoming gift on my arrival to live in Israel. I had never seen one like it before. It told of a fallen pilot, a cousin I had never seen, a 23-year-old member of a Kibbutz, whose plane crashed. I found it difficult to read the book, for it was during the War of Attrition and pictures of fallen soldiers were appearing every day in the newspapers. My own son had been perilously close to a bomb explosion set by terrorists in a residential quarter of Haifa. Still, I kept it on my table and looked at its title, *A Boy Forever*, and at the picture of birds in flight against the cloudy background. On the back cover appears a close-up of three birds. They look as if they have just been hit by a bullet and are appallingly still against the clouds – they are about to plummet to their destruction but temporarily remain frozen.

The book serves as a memorial. It contains a diary my cousin's mother kept while he grew up, and includes letters, short compositions, comments, evaluations and memories written by friends, teachers and relatives. A veritable library of such commemorative literature exists in Israel. The Defense Department has for years employed a well-known Israel author, Reuven Avinoam, to sift through the literary remains of fallen soldiers. He chooses the very best of their writings for the commemorative anthology that is periodically published. To date four such anthologies have appeared. Each volume contains some 600 folio-size pages. The selections comprise poems, letters, compositions and stories, as well as examinations and term papers. Of course, the quality is very uneven, but the overall impact of the volumes is powerful. Many Israeli households contain one or more of these volumes.

But there are thousands of the individual commemorative books. They range in size and elaborateness from professionally written, designed, printed, bound publications, to mimeographed, stapled sheets. The Defense Department budget includes funds to assist bereaved families wishing to publish such a book – hardly surprising, then, that there are so many.

The contents of the memorial book are quite uniform, but such books have some distinctive features worthy of note. Take for instance, one of the earliest, a trilogy about Shmuel Kaufman and Zahara Levitov, fiancés, who were killed in the 1948 war. The story of their heroism in 1948, he as a membr of the Palmach, and she as the first woman pilot in the fledgling Israeli Air Force, and of their young love, is brilliantly told. Their book contains many of the themes repeated in later ones. It includes the idea that death is not a matter for the dead and dying alone, but also for those whose lives are intertwined with them and with their hopes for the future. And it includes literary remains as well as appreciative statements by friends and relatives.

The real purpose of this and other commemorative books is to present "a spiritual picture of a special young being who lives his life in the light of a dream and vision." Cosmic, transcendent, foreordained qualities often are ascribed to the death: "While he was still in the hospital beside his mother, it seemed as if from heaven they came to snatch him; on the 11th of the month of Tammuz, 3:30 in the afternoon, there were severe earth tremors."

In many of these books there is strong identification with the national memories and aspirations of the Jewish people. For example, the soldier as a young child "would say to his sister, 'Father has books in Hebrew, English and Greek.' When asked: 'What is Greek?' he answered, 'The language of the Greeks that destroyed our temple.' " And as a young boy of fifteen seeking consolation when his mother died, he found it in national aspirations: "'It is a weighty question: what consolation can we find (for our mother's death)... the answer lies in Zionist exertion and working for our homeland.' "

The painfully tragic story of young love frequently appears, as in the Kaufman Levitov biography: "They read together in their holy temple during a leave they both had from the army. They read poetry, they loved each other and listened to classical music." "It seemed to me" [writes the father] "that they were elevated to heavenly spheres in their mutual love." And finally, the plans for the future: a university education and... marriage.

Subtle differences occur between themes and ideas expressed in the earlier commemorative literature (written in the period around 1948) and those in books written during the Six-Day War and after. Most interesting is the status of war. The pacifistic values of the late 1960's worldwide youth culture filtered through to Israeli youth. The most blatant manifestation of these values in Israel following the Six-Day

War was the well known "letter of the twelfth graders." The letter challenged both prevailing assumptions about the inevitability of war with the Arabs and the government's willingness to make peace. During this same period a stage presentation, *The Queen of the Bathtub*, satirized patriotism and the zeal to engage in war. It was finally removed from the stage because of the outraged public reaction.

Memorials for soldiers during the later period show them wrestling with these difficult moral choices. The commemorative book for David Uzan, who was killed at the age of nineteen at the Suez Canal May 23rd, 1970, includes a letter he wrote from a bunker on the Bar Lev line at the Canal to a friend in Switzerland. "Enough Mickey, enough!... Have you thought of what a boy my age does who lives in Europe?... He is demonstrating for progressive Socialism, against the Establishment. For the love of freedom, against the war in Vietnam, for the free distribution of birth control pills in the University, against Zionism and Imperialism, anti-everything... Anti. For nothing positive only for the anti. Can anything be better? And what does a fellow my age in Israel do? If you don't know I will tell you – he guards the borders of his country... and here I am in a few months about to celebrate my twentieth birthday... but I do not envy the European rebel. He leads a boring life by comparison and one without any worthy end."

In his published letter we find a new moral wrestling, the same one that one finds in the *The Seventh Day* edited by Avraham Shapira. It is not enough to fight and die for one's country. A soldier must respond to questions. The introspective side of Israeli character is more revealed in memorial literature than anywhere else.

In Israel the dead are memorialized with a passion not only in the ways I have mentioned but in others as well. The country includes nineteen sturdy structures dedicated to dead soldiers, hundreds of memorial rooms in settlements of all kinds (kibbutzim, moshavim, development towns, schools, etc.) The papers overflow with notices of memorial gatherings and conferences. The dead of all Israel's history have found a visible memorial in Israel. Israel remembers its dead as few societies do.

Each spring a series of memorial days bring most of the Jewish population of Israel to a fever of passionate memorializing activity. Holocaust and Heroes Day, with its stark realism, is followed by Jerusalem Day, which perpetuates the memory of those who died reuniting Jerusalem. These are followed by Remembrance Day, for all of Israel's war dead, Independence Day close on its heels. During a period of slightly more than one month four public holidays commemorate the dead and their valor. Each of them has powerful symbols that gain significance in institutionalized settings and that are effectively communicated by the mass media.

It is certainly hard to remain indifferent when sixty sets of parents, each of whom has lost at least two sons in combat, light a lamp of remembrance at the Western Wall, or when the sirens sound in the morning and the entire country stands at attention in silent tribute, or when viewing on television interviews with the little children of fallen soldiers. No effort is spared to sharpen the memory, to make one aware of the sacrifice. In short to make the dead relevant to the living. There are some, such as the writer A. B. Yehoshua, who see in the preoccupation with death the distinguishing characteristic of Israeli society.

What is the impact of these hundreds of memorials and the thousands of books? It is so great that some critics stand in awe of it. Leah Ben Dor comments: "Mourning is a tradition for the Jews, and no wonder, there has been too much opportunity to practice it, too many who have died before they had run their span. It is in danger of becoming a substitute religion." What an apt description of the Israeli scene. Every society has its deaths, ordinary deaths. But when have there been so many heroes?

Perhaps of all the peoples existing in the world Israelis best understand the character in Elton John's "Old Soldier" who says: "Well do they know what it's like to have a graveyard as a friend, Cos that's where they are boy, all of them. Doesn't seem likely I'll get friends like that again." It is another of the tragic realities of the Jewish people that in Israel so many of the population are preoccupied with monuments and graveyards as friends. It is perhaps gratifying that finally there are Jewish heroes, but the terrible reality is that they are dead. These celebrations are one way of handling that tragedy.

C. Retrieving the Living: Israeli Reaction to Bereavement in War

By the second week of the Yom Kippur War it was clear that the surprise attack from many fronts and the ongoing defense and counterattacks had already cost many casualties and many deaths. To cope with this crisis the government recruited all social workers not working in war-related or emergency services. They were to perform crisis intervention work with the bereaved families. Immediately after a family received notification of a death, they were to visit to assess its capacity to cope and to offer concrete services.

Concrete Services

Few workers or families would dispute the need for concrete services. Although some bereaved families express hurt at the suggestion that they may wish to benefit financially from their tragedy, these same families generally agree that it is a good idea for others. The reactions vary greatly. Widows generally do not question their right to income support; society assumes that a husband's role is to support his wife, and thus income maintenance is usually taken for granted. When it comes to parents who have lost a son, and for members of collective kibbutz the issue is more delicate. Concrete services can here be a source of embarrassment and confusion.

During the twenty-five years prior to the Yom Kippur war, Israel developed an extremely intricate and humane set of concrete services to which each family is entitled. Widows receive a monthly income from the Rehabilitation branch of the Defense Ministry for as long as they live, unless they remarry. The government guarantees children of fallen soldiers all educational costs through University. Parents receive payments according to their need, as well as the right to various rehabilitative loans. All these rights and many more are covered in a booklet, and one of the social worker's tasks is to tactfully place the booklet in the home of the family for perusal when they are capable of reading it.

Every family is affected differently, and in a situation of massive intervention the timing of services cannot be sufficiently based on differential diagnosis. Some families are reached too soon, while still in deep shock and not ready to relate, and others are not reached soon enough. Feelings of neglect, anger and hurt may have developed which are difficult to overcome. In some families the need for concrete services is intense and the worker is flooded with specific requests which may take a long time, if ever, to fulfill. Other families resent the concreteness of the services offered and seek a more personal, verbal interaction.

Furthermore, a professional working with a population that has been struck by catastrophe is not immune to the impact of that catastrophe. The worker who starts out on a day's journey with a list of bereaved families to visit and to relate to must return to the privacy of her own fears for her family.

The Limits of a Worker's Understanding

A temporary crisis intervention worker's goals when visiting the bereaved family are to size up the situation, empathize with the family, find whatever immediate problems need handling, communicate the situation to the permanent worker of the region, recommend concrete services or any other follow up deemed necessary, and predict the possible course of recovery or deterioration.

Of course, those who work with bereaved families hope intensely that those who have been struck by tragedy are strong. Israel is a small country and there is not a family which does not have a son, father, husband, brother, daughter or cousin in a place of danger when there is a war. The need to paint a rosy picture is sometimes overwhelming.

Nonetheless, some families are so completely devastated by the death that their disintegration cannot be denied. There are families who have lost the person whose role in the family structure was crucial, around whom all organization revolved. When such a person suddenly dies, their loss brings both grief, which is universal, and a paralysis which is somewhat more rare.

The limited capacity of the worker in such a situation to grasp the reality of loss to individuals within the family is particularly clear to the family. In a situation of massive intervention the sensitivity of the worker's perception is difficult to maintain, and the worker may report that a family is strong. What does this mean? How many "strong" families then sink into deep depression or suicide? On the other hand, there are situations where the worker will err to the other extreme and report deep pathology where there is actually an understandable acute grief.

The Right to Intervene

Does a temporary worker have a right to intervene in a family's grief? Some families anticipate the visit of a worker – either from experience with friends or because it seems appropriate to them that their loss should have formal recognition and acknowledgement. If the worker is sensitive to their need to share grief, they will use the visit to talk. But are they aware that the possibility for a return visit by the same worker is slight unless they have the strength to specifically request it? Has the family been helped by beginning a relationship and ending it in one short hour? Would it be better not to visit at all? What does this situation do to the worker's sense of values? Can we maintain our sense of professional integrity and avoid succumbing to the pull of a volunteer "friendly visitor" routine? Did we do great harm in those first six weeks as we wandered dazedly from one family to another? I myself visited over forty families! What happened to differential diagnosis and treatment during those first intensive weeks?

And what happens to a perpetual intake worker during a period of massive intervention in a specific crisis? Where does the treatment phase come in? Can we maintain a separation between intake and treatment for a worker and still maintain the tools for effective intervention? Does not the intake assessment tool become dulled when differential treatment seems hopelessly unavailable because of the limited backup resources?

It is rare for the specific needs of a bereaved individual and the specific approach of a particular worker to coincide. But at such moments there is the possibility for significant positive intervention.

Three Alternatives

The worker who knocks at the door of a bereaved Israeli family must make several decisions during the first minutes of her stay. She may decide to relate to an individual member of the family. Sometimes it is a brother, or the mother-in-law, or even a silently grieving girlfriend in a kibbutz. She may plan to treat the family as a whole and be drawn into a web of unresolved interpersonal problems originating in the distant past. She may see the family as part of the common tragedy that struck the whole country, being mesmerized by that collective pain and, therefore, unable to function in any normal responsible way.

The worker's three choices correspond roughly to the three states a bereaved person might believe himself to be in. A person may feel himself isolated and unique in his or her grief. Nobody can understand him; neither his partner nor his parents can fathom the depth of his misery. He shuts himself off from any contact with his surroundings, unable to permit himself or somebody else the luxury of a moment's relaxation. He craves a mystical unity with the fallen. All his grief and anger are turned inward; a rigid shell surrounds him through which no feeling or thought connecting him with either the world outside or the beloved person inside is allowed to penetrate. He cannot liberate his grief.

Conversely, one may become subject to heavy pressures from various members of the family. Death can suddenly change one's place in the family constellation – a brother becomes an only child; a young wife becomes the widow whose in-laws seem to want to wrest from her the few things reminding her of her husband; or a caring mother is accused by her husband of gross neglect of the family. All these people are being crushed under the burden of an uncomprehended tragedy, too weak to resist the various forces acting upon them. They cannot tune their ears to and focus their eyes on the other members of the family; they send endless nonverbal messages crying for help and support.

Finally, some people feel they have surrendered to a common fate. They have rejected all responsibility for their own actions and fate. Some undefined, terrible machine has killed their beloved, and it is that same force that has assumed the responsibility for providing them with almost anything they want. They transform Hell into some sort of distorted paradise in which they are cared for without any effort on their part.

Perspectives for Workers With the Bereaved

When a worker reaches out to another human being in a professional way there are three ways in which she can find contact with the one needing her help.

As a professional, the worker will use all her knowledge, sociology, social work, psychology, anthropology, etc. She will explore the social and economic forces functioning in a family, the conscious and unconscious wishes of its members, and the inclinations of each individual. She will listen, constantly forming or rejecting hypotheses and offering suggestions. She will attempt to guide each individual toward a better understanding of the motives and needs governing the lives of those surrounding him. She will also try to avoid pronouncing judgement or evaluating behavior. She must refrain from manipulating her clients for the benefit of some third party. Her task is not to turn the client into a good wife, husband, soldier or citizen. It is not her business to suppress genuine anger or aggressiveness toward a person or institution. Her sole concern is with helping the stricken person to function in a responsible, independent way, according to the realities of his situation.

The worker as administrator is the technician of this triad. She is concerned with vital, practical functions such as finances, and the smooth functioning of the individual in the bureaucracy of agencies, arm and state. She will pick up the broken threads connecting the individual and his surroundings.

As philosopher, the worker will try to open wider horizons and explore with the bereaved such difficult questions as the meaning of life, death and suffering. She will find contact through discussion, exploration, self-exposure and explanation.

When the worker can combine all three qualities while caring for her client, she may succeed in helping the victims of war. By blending the three perspectives she has become more than a worker. She has become a creative human being.

There are people who do not need us – those faced with stark, naked misery and the most profound desolation and those with the inner strength to take fate in their own hands. In those cases, the worker is left with a fourth possible decision – to leave humbly, closing the door silently behind her, with the liberating feeling of not having rushed in where angels fear to tread.

D. Death: A Threat to War's Legitimacy

A nation at war that wants civilian support for its fight and soldiers for its battles must acknowledge that soldiers get killed. Thus, any military establishment that wishes to fulfill its function must actively respond to bitter accusations from bereaved families. One such Israeli family published this following vengeful lament after their son died in the Lebanon War:

> Raviv, to your fresh grave I have come.
>
> In the name of all those responsible for the event
>
> I have come to ask forgiveness.
>
> I ask your forgiveness for the Defense Minister
>
> who made the hasty decision to storm unoccupied Beirut.
>
> I ask your forgiveness for the Division Commander
>
> who threw your Nahal brigade into battle precipitously
>
> I ask your forgiveness in the name of your battalion commander
>
> who sent two young tank commanders out on a singular and difficult mission,
>
> I ask your forgiveness in the name of the Brigade commander of the Nahal who conducted the battle in an incompetent manner,
>
> I ask your forgiveness in the name of the Zev, the tank commander who fled from the battle and abandoned a friend in dire straits.
>
> I ask your forgiveness for the Captain who was to bring reinforcements, who didn't trouble himself or endanger himself to provide the support you needed.
>
> I ask your forgiveness for all those Nahal officers in the rear lines who didn't extend themselves to evacuate the wounded from the cave.
>
> I ask forgiveness, as it is written in the liturgy on the Holy Days of Awe:
>
> "And for all these Sins, Forgive us, Forgive us,
>
> Have compassion upon us, and Exonerate us."

If the military wishes to retain its legitimacy for military personnel and civilians alike it *must* address the devastating sense of loss felt by relatives and friends of fallen soldiers. Resources must be found and procedures implemented to help those who experience the death of a loved one. The death must be explained in a way that is understandable and acceptable – or at least minimally so. But that is not enough. The death also must be officially acknowledged and commemorated. It has to be placed within rational and publically recognized frameworks; it has to be legitimated.

The notion of legitimate death in war is based on a belief that somehow the causes behind the hostilities are fundamentally correct: the war being fought is for a morally justifiable cause; it is being pursued by those who are authorized to lead the nation in arms; they are active with some degree of competence. These are the beliefs that help justify the personal sacrifice necessary in armed struggles. But these beliefs, when they exist, are just abstractions for most people. When tragedy hits home and a loved one is killed in war the psychic cost of maintaining these abstract beliefs becomes painfully real. Belief in the legitimacy of life sacrifice can be severely challenged, and the resulting second thoughts about the war can deeply affect the war's conduct.

When thoughts about the worth of sacrifice remain within the private realm and the limited circles of bereaved relatives and friends, there is no immediate threat to the overall public legitimization of war. But when those reservations run rampant and become public issues, they call into question the very purposes that impel nations to fight and maintain armies. Particular wars and the military institutions that support them risk losing legitimacy when this happens.

Their crisis may be concretely expressed in a variety of ways: the fighting troops lose morale; the public at large becomes unwilling to allocate resources towards the pursuit of hostilities. And the strength of these factors can cause armies to cease functioning as effective fighting units. Thus in all armies and societies the poorly explained, incompetently commemorated military death constitutes a potential catalyst for a crisis of legitimacy.

The Israeli Situation

In this essay we intend to deal briefly with Israel's response to the fallen soldier. We must point out that while many of the specific issues met by the Israeli military arise for other nations and other armies, not all do.

A number of factors have coalesced to make the military's handling of bereavement particularly important in Israel. First, many Israeli families have been traumatized by memories of the Holocaust – either directly or indirectly. For those families including concentration camp survivors, the strength of the Israeli army acts as a necessary compensation for those feelings of hopelessness and impotence that were their lot as camp victims. Losing a relative or a friend in war calls that strength into question, so during moments of bereavement the camp victim's characteristic sense of hopelessness and their impotent rage return.

Predictably, the 250,000 camp inmates now living in Israel are particularly mindful of the horrors of death. For them, the loss of a loved one frequently triggers a whole world of horrible associations that are barely under control in the best of circumstances. Their feelings for their children reach beyond those shared by all parents; they are tinged with the notion that these children are surrogates for relatives who died in horrible circumstances. Children in Israel bear the heavy emotional burden of standing in for millions of dead uncles, aunts and grandparents who perished at the hands of the Nazis. When these children themselves are killed, the anguish and bitterness of surviving parents and relatives is overwhelming. And indeed the recency of the Holocaust creates an aura of tragedy which pervades the entire society and reinforces the bereaved individual's sense of loss – even when he or she has no direct Holocaust experience.

Second, the incessant wars since 1948 have created for Israelis a permanent condition of exposure to death in battle. Some 12,000 individuals have died in war for Israel since the State came into being. In 1947-49, 558 soldiers and 1,100 civilians were killed; during the border skirmishes and campaigns of retribution, 1,138; the Sinai Campaign, 176; while serving in the border patrol and military police, 759; in the Six-Day War, 789; the War of Attrition, 669; the Yom Kippur War, 2,686; the Lebanon War, over 700. There are some 18,000 bereaved families in Israel, including some 3,500 war widows.

Further, because Israel has a citizen army, virtually every household has individuals who are exposed to the dangers of war. The average Israeli male spends some seven years in active service between the ages of eighteen and fifty-four, and that not infrequently in combat circumstances. And all Israelis are exposed to the constant threat of terrorist attack. The large numbers of terrorist attacks, bombings and killings mean that bereavement is always potentially on the agenda both for families and for the society at large. Death due to hostilities, is ubiquitous in Israel. It has been ever since 1929.

The relatively small size of the population and the particularly close knit nature of the society mean that many people will know those who have been killed. There is thus a constant danger of resentment, panic and despair becoming epidemic. If one asks a random group of Israelis how many have lost an immediate relative or close friend in the hostilities, one finds that more than half of those older than eighteen have been bereaved. By comparison, it was not uncommon during the Vietnam War for complete segments of the American public to have had no contact with bereaved families (this even though more than 50,000 American soldiers were killed). Indeed, many subgroups among Americans actually had no friends or relatives who served in the army. This is inconceivable in Israel.

Moreover until now, most of Israel's wars have brought fighting close to its population centers. Consequently people feel involved in what happens on the battle lines. Death is not isolated geographically – it is not something that happens in some remote "over there." In Israel it is "here and now." This geographical proximity also influences how soldiers react to family deaths on the home front. The fortunes of those at home and in battle are potentially reciprocal because there is a high degree of communication between home and battle lines. Indeed, it is not uncommon for families to have "representatives," generally friends, relatives or neighbors, on every front who keep them informed about their loved ones. In future wars, fighting units may even have their own "representatives" on the home front – particularly if that home front is going to be subject to bombardment, which seems likely.

There is no significant geographic distance between the front and the home, so hardly any time at all lapses between a disaster's occurrence and its becoming common knowledge. Informal networks of communication among Israelis see to that. On occasion, informal and militarily illegal forays of civilians have been known to go to the front looking for missing relatives. Consequently the Israeli military has had to develop a fast and accurate system to keep its citizens informed about losses in battle. Unless the military acts fast it is highly likely that the informal means of communication in Israel's tightly knit society will preempt those military communication channels set up to deal with notification of loss of life. The chances of inaccurate reporting are greater through informal communication channels.

The army authorities in Israel do everything in their power to be the first to get to the family with the bad news because when the army does not present the circumstances surrounding the death first, the credibility of its explanation is significantly lowered. Even though the authorities in the Israeli military are well aware that "the bringer of unwelcome news hath but a losing office, and his tongue sounds ever after as a sullen bell," they realize it would be more sullen still if it did not fulfill its responsibility as first conveyer of the news, bad as it is.

And the deeply humanistic value placed on individual life in Israeli society makes the loss of the single soldier a major event not only for the family involved but for the society at large. Indeed, during her term as Prime Minister prior to the Yom Kippur War, Golda Meir reportedly instructed her military aide to wake her if an Israeli soldier died in combat while she slept.

Thus the death of every soldier diminishes everyone in peculiarly intense ways. Not only is an individual lost, Israelis fear that their country is demographically diminished by any death. Jews consider themselves a struggling minority. One third of the Jewish people were destroyed in World War II, and the Jews of Israel are outnumbered by the surrounding Arab population more than thirty times over. So in addition to Israelis' concern for human life they experience intense anxiety in case their population should shrink.

Not surprisingly, then, the high incidence of death and maiming in Israeli society as a result of hostilities during the past thirty-eight years has made bereavement a matter of utmost importance to the military. It has potentially disruptive political and military effects. These effects became actualized following the Yom Kippur War in 1973-74. At that time, bereavement helped to energize a mass political protest movement which resulted in the fall of the Labor government after twenty-six years of power. Moshe Dayan, the Defense Minister at the time, was regarded by the public at large as responsible for Israel's being caught unprepared and for the resulting heavy loss of life. He could hardly appear in public without being angrily accosted by scores of bereaved parents.

Israel's attitude to fallen soldiers is much influenced by Jewish religious and cultural tradition. It is this tradition and its values which have guided the establishment of military bereavement procedures.

Jewish tradition is realistic, ritualistic and constructionist in regard to death and bereavement. It is realistic in its assessment of the profound depths of human emotion associated with loss. It makes no attempt to inhibit the full expression of highly personal and individualized emotions evoked by bereavement. In fact it allows them free rein within rather broadly defined limits. Bereaved persons are licensed to express their pain and anguish in whatever way they wish. There are few if any sanctions against "giving in to one's emotions" at a time of bereavement. It is expected behavior.

The codified norms of the Jewish legal tradition caution that a person seeking to comfort a mourner should not ask how the person feels. It is an idle question. There is no way for the mourner to describe the feeling of loss unless they spontaneously choose to do so. Indeed, visitors to the home of mourners are encouraged to speak only if the mourner wishes to. If the mourner wishes to laugh the visitor is encouraged to join in if possible; if the mourner wishes to speak, the visitor is encouraged to follow the lead and speak. But in the face of death, the most eloquent comment is sometimes silence itself.

Jewish tradition assumes that mourning is a very individual affair, and that each person mourns in their own way. It is the task of those who wish to offer comfort to do so in a way that is responsive to the flow of emotions from the mourner. Since these emotions are unpredictable, the visitor is to take his or her lead from the mourner. Emotional expression is the expected behavior, but the form that expression takes is individual.

The Jewish tradition is ritualistic in that it prescribes behavior according to the passage of time. It assumes that mourning requires time to run its psychological course. The "working through" process is delineated ritualistically. Carefully stipulated ceremonials guide the mourner through four defined mourning periods. First, there are rules to guide behavior in the period before burial. A second set of rules guides behavior after the burial through seven days of mourning. During these days the mourner stays at home and is available to the friends and relatives of the deceased. The third set of rules relates to behavior until thirty days have passed after the death. The fourth set relates to behavior up to the conclusion of the first eleven months.

How is the Jewish tradition constructionist? It uses the mourning period to achieve prescribed social goals. Mourning provides an occasion to strengthen family ties, and to gather networks of friends, relatives and groups to which the deceased belonged. It is an occasion for giving funds to institutions and worthy causes that the deceased supported. These secondary gains of mourning situation strengthen the group. Families are reunited in their moment of sorrow. Groups are strengthened because their members have to reassess the group's aims in light of the void created by the death of one of its members. In material terms, social institutions gain through the contributions given in the name of the deceased. Thus the secondary gains of mourning and bereavement are intrinsically constructionist. They reinforce and support the structures of society.

The military in Israel has wisely decided to take cognizance of these religious and cultural traditions and to adapt itself accordingly. Consequently the services it renders to families are themselves realistic, ritualized and constructionist. A woman who is notified that her husband has been killed needs someone to look after her children until she can begin to function properly; the army will pay for a babysitter. She may need someone to help her explain to her children that their father has been killed; the same person who notified her frequently will stay and help her tell them.

The services are also ritualized, and they vary within different time frames. The memorial department does not immediately arrive to help the mourning family collect the literary memorabilia for a memorial book – it waits until the time is ripe. The social worker who provides information about financial help which the Defense Department extends to the bereaved also appears at the appropriate time.

Finally, army support is constructionist; it tries to make the best of what is a tragedy for the family. It tries to organize peer support groups from others similarly stricken, and within the bounds of good taste it attempts to celebrate the heroism and moral virtues of the fallen soldier in order to strengthen the society's resolve and morale.

Rabbis are involved in the soldier's death from the beginning. The chief Rabbi of the Israeli army actually has a helicopter at his disposal and oversees a large staff of field Rabbis who are with troops in combat. Those that search the battlefield for the dead are associated with the Chevra Kadisha, "the Holy Society." They care for the body once it is located; they are involved in the identification. And once the body is released by the medical authorities, they are responsible for all subsequent procedures. For instance, they cooperate to prevent families from seeing the remains of their fallen soldier, for the sight of a dear one's demolished body can leave a scar for life. And the military's religious authorities participate in the pre-burial rituals such as purification and preparation of the body for burial. Together with the Regional Army Officer, known in Israel as "the Officer of the City" (Ktzin HaIr), they take responsibility for the burial and mourning rituals. They bring the body to the cemetery, prepare the grave and help the family arrange their home for the mourning ritual. Indeed, the religious functionaries have a say in organizing the house of mourning.

Throughout, they are available for consultation and for support. They have continuous contact with the family, not only during the eleven months of mourning but for the yearly anniversary of the death and during the special commemorative days for years to come after the tragedy. There is a very close relationship in Israel between the military and religious authorities, a relationship that is rarely challenged even by the most secular of Israel's Jews. (For non-Jewish groups in Israel who are involved in the military, such as the Druze and the Bedouin, virtually all arrangements for burial and mourning are conducted by the religious authorities of their own communities.)

Military Practice: Humane Treatment

Bereavement practices in the Israeli military are much influenced by their military context. The army institutionalizes its procedures in ways typical of hierarchical, bureaucratic organizations. Military regulations guiding the behavior of personnel are as predetermined as circumstances allow; as little as possible is left to chance. Every effort is made to foresee all possible contingencies and to learn from past mistakes. In dealing with the issue of fallen soldiers the army is dealing with a situation *in extremis,* where the smallest mistake or impropriety reverberates for a long time. Mistakes by military personnel can result in official censure.

At the burial of a young soldier emotions are raw. By its very nature the situation is emotionally volcanic. Bitterness and anger are almost always on the verge of bursting the bounds of restraint. In order to avert violent emotional outbursts, the military has devoted resources to "cool out" (Erving Goffman's phrase) those individuals who have suffered the most grievous loss that wars impose, the loss of a spouse, parent, child, brother, other relative or friend. I do not mean to infer that these mechanisms indicate the Israeli military lacks compassion for the sufferings of the individual bereaved. From my own work with the Psychological Division of the Israeli army I have observed that the opposite is most frequently the case. But I do stress that bereavement occasioned by the death of combatants is a problem for the military on the institutional level.

In a free and democratic society, as we have noted, if the military does not deal with bereavement successfully the resentment generated by unrestrained grief has widespread political effects and prevents military institutions from doing what they are designed to do: making war. How so? Armies depend on allegiance and assent. These qualities are vulnerable; they are open to influence by contagious emotions. And since few human emotions are as intense or as volatile as those connected with death and mourning, if the army is to continue fighting it must help the bereaved to deal with their feelings.

How does an army actually achieve this?

In Israel, the army and certain adjunct offices of the defense department have assumed responsibility for the following tasks:

1. identification of the deceased
2. care for the body until burial
3. notification of the immediate family
4. caring for the physical and psychological well being of the relatives

5. making arrangements for the funeral
6. planning and performing the ceremony at the grave site
7. helping the family with the necessary ritual articles for the house of mourning
8. administering miscellaneous services accorded to families by the defense department and the army, including: arranging medical aid; providing financial aid for funeral and mourning expenses; notifying family members abroad; making arrangements for bringing to the funeral immediate family who happen to be abroad at the time of the death, coordinating visits by the dead soldier's commanding officer and members of his army unit to the bereaved family
9. making sure that army personnel are available to the family during the seven days of mourning

Two weeks after the funeral the army authorities, as represented by the "Officer of the City," hand over their responsibilities to the staff of the Defense Department's social service rehabilitation unit. The rehabilitation staff provides a variety of services to the family. In particular, they offer generous financial support for widows and children. Some consideration is given to other members of the family as well. For example surviving only brothers of fallen soldiers are exempted from serving in combat units. There are therapeutic facilities for family members who need them, and subventions for the purpose of purchasing apartments and cars. Financial assistance is available for convalescence. Other services include help during the immediate period of mourning and during the subsequent period of rehabilitation. All families receive a monthly allowance. Children of the fallen get help in meeting educational expenses through college. Other services deal with ceremonial means of perpetuating the memory of the fallen soldiers. These include the organization of days of remembrance, the construction and consecration of suitable war memorials, the publication of books of remembrance, and many other kinds of memorial activities.

In this brief summary, which is by no means exhaustive, I have hurried through what is, in actuality, a vast corpus of regulations and procedures that are implemented by thousands of army and civilian personnel in a sizable bureaucratic structure.

When the system works, it works very well. When it doesn't, all hell breaks loose. One then witnesses death's awesome potential to create havoc in the military.

Outrage over the mishandling mobilizes vast public energies. The overall impact is analogous to a failed theodicy in the history of a religion. When God fails religion goes through a crisis because there is no convincing explanation as to how the God of the group can allow defeat and tragedy to happen to the pious faithful. Civilizations, societies and religions are destroyed when theodicies chronically fail to provide satisfactory explanations for disaster. When they do their work, the greatest of disasters fail to lower the group morale.

The best example of this situation is the way theodicy succeeded among the Jews after the destruction of the second Temple in the year 70 C.E. Disaster and destruction were all around, but the people were kept going because they believed they were being punished for their sins. Their failures occurred not because their God had deserted them, but rather because they had sinned in the eyes of God.

Not surprisingly, armies are in the business of keeping people "cooled out" about fallen soldiers.

Some Case Studies

The following brief synopses of specific cases reveal concretely how the system works.

Case Study One: When the System Works Well

Zev died in a tank during the Lebanon War. His body was found intact; his identification tags were where they should be. First, his body was brought to the hospital in the Northern part of Israel, where it was identified. His tank's destruction was witnessed by other soldiers, so the details of his death could be reported to the proper army authorities. They gave the authorization to notify Zev's parents.

The notification team was headed by a high army officer (a person known for his compassion and ability to speak to people). As for the team's other members, they were a physician and a psychologist. They had been on standby orders for just this kind of an assignment for two weeks.

Their first task was to gain entry into the apartment house without arousing the neighbors (who would know what kind of news three uniformed army officers might be bringing to the family). They notified the parents, who were home at the time. No one needed medication. Then they stayed with the family for two hours – until family members arrived from other parts of the city.

Next morning, at the funeral, representatives from the son's unit formed the honor guard. And toward the end of the seven days of mourning, Zev's battalion commander came to the house to explain the particular circumstances in which Zev was killed, and just why the battle in which he had died was important.

Then the family collected all the letters that Zev had written to them from the army, as well as those he had written to his girlfriend Zahava. A few friends who had been in school with him contributed essays about him, and with the help of the Defense Department the family published a memorial book in his honor. Each Remembrance Day the parents, together with Zahava and Zev's friends, visit his grave. The Defense Department has been helping Zev's parents in various ways over the years to help them bear their financial and psychological burden.

Case Study Two: The Wrong One is Notified

"Yoram" died during a defensive action. He was killed in an army unit to which he had just been assigned. No one in the unit had met him before he became part of it, so identification was made through tags found on the body. When the notification team came to the house to tell the family that Yoram had been killed, however, the mother shouted out that Yoram wasn't dead; on the contrary, he was home and in the shower. The notification team's head waited for Yoram to finish his shower and asked him how his tags had come to be found on the body of a dead soldier. Apparently, Yoram's brother Baruch had been called up and had taken Yoram's identification tags. It was Baruch who had been killed. (Variations of this episode, which is an actual event, have happened in all of Israel's wars. Some have happier endings.)

Case Study Three: The Suicidal Father

Tzvi belonged to a particularly elite unit, one involved in a secret mission. He had volunteered for the unit and the mission because there was a tradition of military bravery in the family. Both the father, who had been in a concentration camp, and the other two sons, had distinguished themselves in various wars. The Officer of the City (The Katzin Ha-ir) knew that the father was a little unbalanced because of his own army and camp experiences, so he sent a psychiatrist with the notification team. And when the family was notified of the son's death, the father made a lunge for the window of his seventh-floor apartment. He was restrained, and army personnel stayed with him for a number of days until he had recovered from the initial stages of his grief. But two months later he was found dead on his son's grave. He had shot himself.

Case Study Four: Whose Negligence?

Five years ago Yochanan, who served in an army unit, decided to light the boiler to heat the water that his army unit needed. The boiler exploded. Someone had placed gasoline in the boiler instead of kerosene. He was burned to death. The army came to notify the family of the accident. After a thorough investigation of all those in the unit it was not clear who had placed the gasoline in the boiler. It could have been Yochanan himself. The father thought that this was impossible. Since that date, in spite of all the army can do to restrain the father, he has been engaged in a virtually full time job of speaking to all the members of the son's unit in order to ascertain the truth. This has gone on for the past five years.

Case Study Five: Perpetual Mourning

Yossi died on the Suez canal during the War of Attrition fifteen years ago. Since that time Yossi's family has devoted itself to finding appropriate memorials for him. They are convinced that his life was exemplary and that if all of Israel's youth knew it Israel would be a healthier society.

They have sponsored a yearly conference for educators about Israel's values. It attracts some hundred or so teachers. The family has dedicated six Torah scrolls with Yossi's name on them for various synagogues; they convinced the Minister of the Interior to dedicate a small forest in his honor; they have published four books of remembrances and essays that he wrote in school; they invite all the members of Yossi's graduating class as well as those in his army unit to their house every year on the anniversary of his death; they have convinced their daughter, who had a son, to name her child Yossi; they frequently talk about what Yossi would have been doing now were he alive; they go to all the memorial meetings of the organization for bereaved parents, Yad Labanim; they are presently trying to convince the principal of Yossi's High School to mount his picture on the remembrance wall – and they constantly communicate with the Defense Department about new ways to perpetuate their son's memory.

Case Study Six: Military Hero/Despicable Husband

Baruch died a hero's death. His exploits are known by every school child in Israel. He defended his position for two days against an overwhelming force of enemy tanks and infantry. For this he was posthumously awarded the highest military honors that the State of Israel can give. Not surprising, one might think, that his wife suffered a nervous breakdown on his death. But the two years of therapy paid for by the Defense Department uncovered pathological reasons for her illness. Her marriage had been a living hell. As a result, she was overjoyed to be free of her husband, but filled with guilt for having hated him. Moreover, she had to bear not only her own feelings, but also the weight of posing as the mourning, adoring wife who cherished his memory. It was more than she could bear. For her, the Defense Department organized a special group of war widows. There she could discuss her ambivalent feelings with a clinical psychologist in an environment that was not judgmental and threatening.

Many possible conclusions could be drawn from these case studies. They illustrate the common ways that people respond to tragic human events. We all know people who are destroyed by tragedy, who make mistakes, who build their lives on memories, who find it difficult to face their true feelings. But the point of these case studies is that a military organization must deal with these responses in a humane way in order to protect its own interests. Especially if it is a citizen army based largely on periodically mobilized civilians.

The Israeli military cannot remain what it is, an effective fighting force of mobilized civilians, while ignoring these all too human responses to tragedy. It cannot overlook the suicidal father, the family searching for the negligent, incompetent perpetrator of their son's death, the perpetual mourner, or the tortured wife of the national hero.

The Israeli military cannot overlook them for a number of reasons. First, they and their families are yesterday's, today's and tomorrow's soldiers. Second, without their active support no one would be willing to serve in the army. Every soldier serving in the army watches how it treats them – they could be his parents, wife or child. These people have a moral halo. They have a moral credit in the eyes of society at large, for they have suffered so that it can persist. While "every hero is a bore at last," according to Emerson, it is not the case with bereaved parents. They maintain their special status in the society. They have had their nearest and dearest taken from them so that the society could survive. As long as it does survive it must express its compassion and gratitude. For a society to denigrate the sacrifices made in its name is in some sense to denigrate itself. By paying homage to its war dead it honors itself. By not allowing the loved ones of fallen heroes to lose heart, society bolsters its own courage. By legitimating their sacrifice and making it a bit easier to bear, society legitimates itself in the eyes of its own citizens.

How is this actually to be accomplished? What is the nature of the institution that deals with the bereaved and the psychologically wounded? In modern societies, those institutions available are both bureaucratic and, in the case of the army, hierarchal. Both characteristics present problems.

Bureaucratic Hubris and Human Tragedy

Peter Berger has taught us that the fundamental bureaucratic presupposition is "that there must be an appropriate agency and appropriate procedure for every conceivable problem in the bureaucratically assigned sector of social life" (Berger, Berger and Kellner, 1973). Applying this to bereavement, we consider it moral hubris to assume that a social institution can formulate appropriate procedures to deal with death under every circumstance. Furthermore, it is quite inconceivable that such procedures could be appropriately formulated as orders so that subordinates in a hierarchical structure could or would obey them and successfully carry them out. The human potential for unanticipated response to fundamental life crises is limitless. To assume that one can foresee them all and provide standardized antidotes is itself a kind of pathology.

To exemplify this we would like to quote from the draft of a publication submitted to the army hierarchy by a clinical psychologist. He was concerned about the long range effects of bringing death notices to families on the notifier. The concern is justified, for as Sophocles said long ago, "none love the messenger who brings the bad news." Persistently bringing bad news must have an adverse effect on the self-image of the messenger. What does it do to him when he bears such evil tidings to people and when he must do it in certain forms and under military command?

The clinical psychologist worried that the messenger might faint from anxiety. The advice/prescription/order was as follows: "What should the messenger do with himself – his inner life – when he comes to the family? How should he prepare himself internally? The qualities that the informer generates should be compassion, softness and love. What should the messenger do when he feels inner pressure (anxiety)? He should not forget to breath! He should attend to his own breathing and should breathe deeply and regularly. Breathing thusly should help in overcoming the anxiety (pressure). What should the messenger tell himself? (We all carry on an inner conversation with ourselves.) It will help the messenger if he will tell himself positive things that strengthen him. That strengthen his belief that he conducted himself correctly and helpfully."

Unless these bits of friendly advice are meant in the most suggestive and tentative way, they create visions of a judgmental dope (in Harold Garfinkel's phrase) who, in the process of disseminating compassion, softness and love, is spending his time thinking positive thoughts and concentrating on breathing! It would constitute the grossest caricature of military bureaucracies to imagine all this formulated in "orders." The mind boggles at the thought of such a "dope" telling parents that their son has been killed.

But if bureaucratic rules and orders cannot handle the existential complexity of the human predicament *in extremis*, what can? Berger has provided us with a way to see such tasks in the military. He calls the capacity of some bureaucracies to allow for humane spontaneity, "the capacity to structure actual eruptions of concrete humanity" (Berger, Berger and Kellner, 1973). This is based on the recognition that one needs a respite from the rules in some extreme situations – a respite from the idea that there is an appropriate procedure for every conceivable problem, that there is an appropriate agency, that it is possible to find someone competent to fulfill every function in the bureaucratic universe, that everyone can fit into a category and be thereby dealt with, that there are definite procedures that can or should be applied to all situations, that individuals should be treated anonymously and without distinction.

The reason the system for dealing with fallen soldiers in Israel works is that it wisely mixes bureaucratic regulation and structured possibilities for the eruption of concrete humanity. Every now and then a bereaved parent, widow or child meets a real person when working their way through the bureaucracy. Furthermore, that person is allowed to function within the bureaucratic structure in a way that allows him/her actually to get things done. Among those assigned parts in dealing with the bereaved, the person with a capacity for concrete humanity can both help the bereaved and help prevent crises of legitimacy from erupting. Almost anyone dealing with the bereaved can fulfill that function.

In one of the northern towns of Israel the individual with the most standing in the community is the person who notifies families that their children have been killed. He does it in such a compassionate, feeling way that the relationships he forges with the families in their darkest hour frequently last. But such concrete humanity can erupt anywhere. It could be not only with those who inform families but with those assigned to be masters of ceremonies at funerals, those who are providers of financial services on behalf of the Defense Department, those assigned to help families find a fitting memorial, those who look after the medical well-being of families, or those whose task it is to interpret the rules to bereaved families. In a word, it can erupt anywhere. Where and when it does, great difficulties are avoided.

George Kateb has written about crises of legitimacy and has defined them as follows: they are "deep and widespread feelings and opinions marked by disaffection from or hostility to the constitutive principles and informing spirit of the country's political arrangements... a legitimation crisis need not be a definite thing. It need not be a clearly manifested condition. It could exist without full explicitness, without people knowing how really disaffected or hostile they were. In the past, great political and social convulsions have sometimes come as a surprise to everyone, including the disaffected and hostile. Some incident or opportunity, or some quick sharp change in condition was needed to crystallize and then to energize the sentiments of crises" (Kateb, 1979, p. 692).

We have been arguing that a soldier's death, wherever it occurs, but in Israel in particular, constitutes a sharp change for others that can cause their disaffection from the constitutive principles of military organizations and of societies. In Israel's case, sudden bereavement through active service is handled by the military. And the reason the application of bureaucratic processes for the bereaved has not crystallized and energized a pervasive sense of crisis is that it has consistently allowed for humane interpretation.

Chapter Five

Death and Annihilation: Nuclear Endings

The final essay in this book was originally delivered at a conference on bereavement organized by the defense establishment in May, 1987. It went by the title "Images of Nuclear Death." The Israeli public has not yet developed an awareness of nuclear devastation, and the public debate on relevant nuclear issues has not begun. The talk constituted an effort to break through the massive resistance to dealing with this unthinkable issue.

The ideas which formed the basis of the talk owe much to members of the Wellfleet Psycho-History group, and in particular to Robert J. Lifton, the Wellfleet group coordinator.

In a sense, this paper brings the book full circle − to the issues of non-violence raised during the civil rights struggle of the 1960s and which were foremost in the authors' consciousness when they made the transition from New York to Haifa. With its reflections on war, death and the Jewish people, it is thus an appropriate essay with which to close this book.

Anyone who raises the nuclear issue with the Israeli public bears a heavy responsibility. Military censorship places the subject under taboo. Indeed, there is a policy of ambiguity about the bomb. But there is also a sense in which a nuclear capability seems just too much to deal with. One more problem added to the Israeli population's burden. Nonetheless, the issue has surfaced in a number of recently published books and in current periodicals. The fallibility of experts in the Vanunu, Pollard and Shabak affairs, and the unreliability of technical systems in the Three Mile Island and Chernobyl disasters, make the nuclear threat to the human race impossible to ignore. We all now share responsibility for the future of humanity.

Even nuclear death has a capacity for metaphoric transformation. All reality can be transformed through the metaphoric sensibility of man. He makes roses the symbol for love, colors symbolize happiness or sorrow. But the nuclear explosion seems to possess a unique power. It manifests nature's fundamental particles and forces. But it destabilizes nature's binding forces and turns them into forces of destruction.

A number of images dominate the public imagination about nuclear death. Between these images there is no necessary coherence or contradiction. As with all public images they comprise fact and fantasy, and some appeal most to one group, some to another. They do, however, serve together as a kind of psycho-social presuppositional base from which public discussion starts.

Since Israel is at long last beginning to face the psycho-social implications of a nuclear world, we propose to consider in this paper some of the images of nuclear death that are widespread in the world today. Possibly, by doing so we can understand ourselves a bit better and avoid the excesses that are part of the nuclear worldview.

NOTHING MORE

Robert Oppenheimer introduced this image to the nuclear age. When he saw the first experimental atomic bomb go off in New Mexico, he reached back into Hindu Scripture and quoted the passage that has become an emblem of the nuclear age: "Now I am become Death, the Destroyer of worlds." The image then gained a classical statement in the works of the political scientist Hans Morgenthau, and the Princeton physicist Freeman Dyson. It has become the stock in trade of Harvard psychiatrist John Mack and New York University psychoanalyst Robert Lifton, and has recently received popular expression in the work of Jonathan Schell.

The idea that everything in this world could disappear is overwhelming in its significance. All the striving, all the accomplishments, all the records of human deeds need witnesses to become meaningful. No one would remain to remember what we and everyone else has done – all human achievement would be placed in a totally absurd light.

Only when we step into the void of a future without a past do we realize how important it is for humans to know that *there will be* a future while they are alive. Imagine a devastated world, devoid of humans, with most cities, works of art, books, inventions, institutions destroyed. Not even any more countries, religions, ethnic groups, children – no more death. Everything human would be "no more."

Why is this such a devastating thought?

For four reasons:

1. A great deal of what we do in life has meaning because it has future promise: we raise children, build a career, develop a

skill. We build; we create. When that future is in doubt the importance of what we do is undermined.

2.   Our works have meaning because we hope or believe that they will last, that our buildings, our symphonies, our poems, our books will persist.

3.   They have meaning because we anticipate an audience of those who will appreciate them and value them.

4.   And a great deal of what we value we valorize because it connects us with some reality greater and more encompassing than ourselves. We value our social group, our religion, our ethnic background.

The fact that everything could disappear changes all that we do. There is no future promise, only future absence. Where once there was reality, now there is only void. The present and the past are doomed by a futureless future. Thus the present has to bear the full burden of providing meaning for all activity. The here and now are the only contexts that are believable. All that provides enjoyment and pleasure has to be encapsulated in an ever contracting and fleeting present. Holding the moment, stopping time becomes the major focus. Stepping out of the inexorable and dooming flow of time becomes the goal. And we can achieve it only by transcending reality through drugs, religion or sexual ecstasy.

But there is one other tactic to cope with the potential cataclysm, one which has not received the attention it deserves: the absolutizing of the relative. Under this scheme, we would not need to create things of lasting significance, or to participate with fellow humans in causes and projects larger than ourselves. All such projects would be revealed to us as unbelieveable fantasies and desperate dreams we hold on to in order to grasp for a morsel of meaning. Desperate times, desperate dreams.

Everyone has his or her own vision of meaninglessness in nuclear times; ours is imagining the manuscripts in the National Library, in the British Museum – with no one to read them. No one to admire the Vermeer paintings in the Frick museum, no one to admire the play of light on the maid's face near the open window; no one to read all those marble stones standing so erect to announce the remains of those who once lived... all the world a mausoleum housing dead humanity's ashes. No one left to mourn or to remember the blasted hopes and strivings. Nothingness.

The image of nothingness is the image of the survivor for a devastated world. It is no doubt the most powerful of all the nuclear age images. Eighteen years ago, prior to our aliya, we visited

Katzetnick, the Holocaust survivor and author of the book *House of Dolls*. He was looking intently at the impressive view of the Haifa port. He said that all he saw was destruction. After the Holocaust, whenever he sees human habitation, he can't help reducing it in his imagination to the possibility of rubble. We saw only teeming life and vitality; he said that we do not know.

Those who have known nothingness know how terribly immanent, how possible it is. One heroic Japanese physician, Dr. Hachiya, recalled that in Hiroshima "for acres and acres the city was like a desert, except for scattered piles of brick and roof tile. I had to revise my meaning of the word destruction or choose some other word to describe what I saw." Or in the words of another Hiroshima survivor: "I climbed Hijiyama hill and looked down. I saw that Hiroshima had disappeared... I was shocked by the sight... what I felt then and still feel now I can't explain with words. Of course I saw many dreadful scenes after that – but that experience, looking down and finding nothing left of Hiroshima – was so shocking that I simply can't express what I felt. I could see Koi (a suburb at the end of the city) and a few buildings standing... but Hiroshima didn't exist – that was mainly what I saw – Hiroshima just didn't exist" (Lifton, 1986, p. 23).

In the Israel of today we may be witnesses to a titanic contest of collective will and decision, a contest between the two powerful images of Never Again and Nothing More.

SURVIVAL

Some, like the Soviet Union, who have been devastated by war, or the Swiss, who have built the world's best nuclear shelters, believe nuclear war is survivable.

The Swiss have the world's most highly developed civil defense protection against nuclear attack. Every Swiss knows where his or her underground quarters are and where to find provisions for long term survival in underground shelters. The world above may be devastated and poisoned, but there will be Swiss coming out of holes in the ground when everything is over.

Russia lost more than 20 million in the Second World War and yet survived to witness the overthrow of the Nazi regime. Consequently, Soviet civil defense and military policy founds itself on the theory that the Soviet Union will survive the horrors of nuclear war. This myth of survival enables Soviet military strategies that envision millions of front line troops slain in a nuclear battle in Europe and tens of millions of civilians killed in attacks on Russian cities. While most of the western world lives with the image of Nothing More, the conviction of survival animates the Russian policy of civilian defense against atomic attack. A good many of the Soviet Union's people believe that the cost will be great, but "We Shall Survive."

Closely allied to this image is the idea of Winning. It is a contest in fantasy. Who will be the surviving Adam and Eve procreating couple after the nuclear holocaust? The Russians are convinced that they will be Russian.

The two other variations to the survival image are the Swiss image of preparedness, and a particularly manifest form of nuclear survivalism which is to be found in the U.S.A.

The more malignant form of survivalism manifests itself in the quasi vigilante groups who see in nuclear holocaust an opportunity for the physically strong and "morally pure" to dominate the America that survives. They are preparing for nuclear destruction with a zeal and anticipation that is almost religious. These are the neo-Nazi groups such as the Aryan Nations and The Order. They are survivalists. They position themselves in isolated places, building up their already extensive arsenal of small and not so small weapons (which they diligently practice using), and anticipating the day, their day, of nuclear holocaust. According to their fantasy, they will be the strongest survivors, posed to take over the American government or even the world. Nuclear war will be their special opportunity to realize their Nazi principles. As Lifton points out "it is the joining together of a murderous and apocalyptic political fundamentalism (the Nazi vision of mass murder in the name of an equally apocalyptic fundamentalism and also in the name of regeneration) via an ostensibly powerful and privileged survivor elite" (Lifton, 1986).

THE GREAT PUNCTUATION MARK IN HISTORY

For some Christian fundamentalist groups the nuclear holocaust seems the long awaited purging, cleansing and redeeming punishment which will set things right once and for all. They consider nuclear war the grand apocalyptic opportunity for which the world has waited.

The Pantax Corporation in Amarillo Texas is the site where nuclear weapons are finally assembled. Thus it seems an obvious first-strike target. A Pentacostal preacher whose church is nearby has pointed out that the book of Revelations in the New Testament is "almost an exact description of thermonuclear blasts." He added that "If the Amarillo bomb dropped today it would bother me not one bit. All would happen in a moment (1 Cor. 15:52) For the trumpet shall sound and the dead shall be raised incorruptible and we shall be changed. The whole world would come into a knowledge of Jesus Christ and a complete understanding of his pattern of living, then without doubt, we would have peace" (Lifton, 1986, p. 13).

This view perceives "nuclear belligerence... simply as implementation of God's own design for creation." It regards individuals as mere instruments of Providence whose job is to help the millennium along. As another Christian American preacher said: "We sit here and we're supposed to be quiet? When we're on the winning team! This isn't the Superbowl, man, this is a run for the glory world!" There is here a desperate desire for a "new heaven and a new earth." Rapture and ecstasy are the goals. Nuclear holocaust becomes the agent of realizing the ultimate Christian victory over evil. But this impulse can be found everywhere; it is not limited to the Christian tradition.

Most prominent among the apocalyptic groups, however, are the Christian sects. They have a long tradition of apocalyptic expectations based on New Testament descriptions of Armageddon, which they center on the Middle East. It is doubtful whether the residents of Yokeneam, Mishmar Haemek and Megiddo are aware that their home towns are part of the "end of the world" imaginings of millions of Christians. Indeed, the nature of these Christian's expectations is not known to most Israelis. With the approach of the millennia year 2000, these expectations have been especially heightened.

According to Dr. Yair Bar-El, recently there have been tourists (with no prior messianic delusions or mental illness) who suddenly started taking their clothes off and prophesying in public in Jerusalem. He believes that these people may be suffering from some sort of "Jerusalem Syndrome," a mystical religious experience specific to this city. He and his colleagues have treated some one hundred odd tourists for Messianic or biblical delusions.

With a nuclearized Middle East and the end of the second millennium only thirteen years away, we can expect to see such hysteria in mass proportions. Anyone who knows the history of such hysteria, and of the apocalyptic explosions around the year 1000 can only fear the craziness that will accompany the year 2000 in the holy city of Jerusalem. A nuclearized Middle East will be the magnet for every religious nut in the world. It is patently absurd to think that the rationality of nuclear deterrence can be maintained in an atmosphere such as the one we will be faced with in just a few, short years.

Of course, since the Six-Day War, some Jewish groups have created for themselves great expectations about the Coming of the Messiah. They are busily preparing on the West Bank and elsewhere for the day in which the Messiah will come to redeem the Jewish people. Jewish theology includes very detailed expectations of the "Pangs of the Messiah," the upheaval and destruction to be loosed. Not a few orthodox Jews accept these "Pangs of the Messiah" as a necessary prelude to the final days.

And finally, some Muslim groups have a well-developed ethic of self-sacrifice and bloodshed. Redemption and personal salvation are said to come through the cleansing of death and destruction. The fanatical effectiveness of this ethic we ourselves have experienced in Lebanon and we have seen it operate in the conflict between Iran and Iraq.

Even without such groups as these, there seems a universal predilection to regard destruction as a prelude to creation and development. One doesn't have to be a religious fanatic to regard death as a necessary cleanser. What else was the Nazi program of euthanasia and genetically based killing if not a vision of mass murder in the name of healing and regeneration! There are plenty of secular fanatics around with similar grand visions of regeneration through mass death. The advocates of Kassah!

It is difficult to anticipate the impact of such religious and cultural ideas in "the crunch." They could act as a kind of self-fulfilling prophecy in which the expectation will create the reality. More probably, if a nuclear conflict connected with the Holy Land seems inevitable, it could paralyze political action by short-circuiting rational, prudent processes with an atmosphere of religious hysteria. Decision makers are not immune to religious expectations and imaginings. For indeed, political leaders are often chosen because of their respect for religious convictions. The last two presidents of the United States, Jimmy Carter and Ronald Reagan, have even voiced openly their apocalyptic expectations.

THE INVISIBLE PERIL

War kills and maims its victims. In the past, however, while psychological effects could span generations, those who suffered physically were generally those who had been in or near the combat areas. In nuclear wars, however, both physical and psychological effects are multi-generational. Those exposed to the nuclear blast carry within them the potential for radiation sicknesses. This potential can manifest itself in delayed malignancies; it can affect generations of unborn children in cruel and intolerable ways.

Many of the effects of nuclear exposure are uncharted and mysterious. A new class of humans was created by the A-bomb. In Japan they are called the Hibakusha, those who have been exposed to intolerable doses of radiation. Their illnesses include: leukemia; cancers of the thyroid and stomach; disturbances of the lung, uterus, liver, heart, kidney. These genetic disturbances in their parents provoke enormous anxiety for the Hibakusha Nisei, second generation survivors (children of the bomb). "While there is no positive evidence yet of intergenerational genetic damage from atomic bomb radiation... it will take many generations to verify."

NUCLEAR "NORMALCY"

Here, nuclear death is placed in the context of everything else we know. There is no vast discontinuity between nuclear war and other kinds of war, between the nuclear bomb and other kinds of bombs, between the nuclear era and other human eras in history. This image draws its convincing power from analogy – to the past. Its rationale runs as follows:

1. All war involves death and killing. More than 100 million people have died in wars since the beginning of the twentieth century. Nuclear war is just more of the same, a bit more spectacular, but a continuation of killing people.

2. All bombs cause destruction of some kind. In the Second World War 42,600 civilians were killed and 40,000 houses destroyed during the July 24-30th allied bombings of Hamburg alone. On the 14th and 15th of February, 1945, 1,665 tons of bombs were dropped on Dresden. Twenty-five thousand civilians were killed and 78,000 houses destroyed. On the 9th to the 10th of March 1945, 83,793 civilians died in bombing raids on Tokyo. All this in conventional war. The few hundred thousand people who were killed in Hiroshima and Nagasaki were just more of the same.

3. There have always been terrible weapons around, chemical and biological weapons. They are not necessarily used. Atomic weaponry is just the same.

4. Nuclear weapons are impractical on the battlefield and only prevent the deployment of armies. They are not precision implements of destruction.

This concept of "nuclear normalcy" is the focus for any military establishment that must prepare for nuclear war. Procedures need to be devised for dealing with such a war. What, for instance, should an American soldier wear? According to a document drawn up by Colonel James Stokes, an army psychiatrist, he should wear an ensemble of mask, hood, overgarment, gloves and boots. What is the soldier to do during atomic attack? Get in the MOPP position: the Mission Oriented Protective Posture. This is not what some of the peaceniks advocate: put your head between your legs and kiss your ass good-bye. PHLKAG!

Language can be mobilized to reinforce this dream of nuclear normalcy. The goal is to make mass destruction thinkable and commonplace by using familiar, non-threatening terms for it, terms such as "nuclear exchange" instead of "nuclear holocaust." The verbal image translates the reality almost into gift giving. Bombs are politely "exchanges." And terms such as "first strike," "second strike," "counter force," "counter value" translate war strategies into moves in a game. But game it is for nuclear tacticians and strategists. Very rarely does the true horror of the nuclear situation come through in the technical literature. It is a literature of circumlocution, one that seldom reveals the pain, anguish and horror of nuclear war. One sees only "forces" and "strategies." Robert McNamara, one of the founders of American nuclear policy, was asked what the difference between a tactical nuclear weapon and a strategic one. In a rare moment of humanistic concern he replied with a wry smile, "A strategic weapon is anything that can hit me."

THE SPECIES SELF

We owe this image for the nuclear age to Erik Erikson, who advocates and supports it. All humanity now lives in the shadow of nuclear peril. Through this technological reality, human beings share in ways never before thought possible; humanity now shares the possibility of common extinction. Despite the horror of this thought, it nonetheless offers a possibility and hope for new forms of human inclusiveness. It creates new opportunities for human bonding and identity. In a nuclear world, if the enemy dies I die; if the enemy survives I survive. The nuclear age binds us all to our enemies; our fate is shared.

We are all members of a species on the brink of self destruction. I am not only a Jew, an Israeli, an American by birth, a parent, a grandparent. I am also linked to my fellow humans with a bond that is every bit as strong and important as all of those. Israelis, Arabs, Russians and Americans all share a common enemy. Extinction. We face together the terrible weapons which modern science has created and we must work together if we are not to set in motion actions that will destroy us all.

In the past the notion of the species self was a Utopian ideal. Now it has become a tragic necessity. According to Erikson, while we protest evil in the world and look after our own interests, there is a more inclusive common interest which must subsume our partial identities under the most inclusive one of all, the "Species Self."

Erikson and his students regard this inclusive sense of identity, the Species Self, as the "most fundamental source of hope available to us." Lifton, one of the most outspoken proponents of this idea, is quick to point out that the spread of this Species Self image does not solve particular political disputes or lessen the number of nuclear weapons in the world. But in the long run, a commitment to humanity will transform the world.

THE AWARENESS OF NUCLEAR DEATH IN ISRAEL

Until now, Israel has not had to "live" with the bomb in social psychological terms. It was an issue for experts. Others were thinking and worrying about it. This is no longer the case, and with time it will be less and less so. Preparing the Israeli population for living with the bomb requires us to address some issues that are on the social psychological agenda in Israel, issues with the greatest resonance for the Israeli mind.

1. Psychic Overload

There comes a point when there is simply too much pressure, too many things to worry about. The atomic issue in Israel may be just that one thing too much. Getting through the month, taxes that are among the highest in the world, terrorism, the frequent army reserve service, the children's long army service, the political problems, the occasional tragedy – and also the atomic bomb. That may be too much.

2. Total Destruction

Israelis will have to live with a new idea: the possibility of total destruction. Everything can be destroyed in an all-out nuclear war. The national symbols can be obliterated: the Wall, the universities, the settlements. Everything. Ancient archeological sites can be vaporized.

3. The Psychosis of Living with the Bomb

Atomic weapons offer enormous power. Those who deal with them are subject to their megalomanic lure. The very idea of the weapon can adversely affect people. If those affected actually have access to nuclear weapons or secrets, the potential for harm is great – The Vanunu Syndrome.

4. The Transformation of Moral Discourse

As a self-avowed nuclear power Israel will have to face the moral implications of its safety being purchased with the threat of annihilation for Arab civilian populations. In order for that threat to be credible, significant numbers of people in Israel will have to be engaged in preparations so that a decision to actually drop the bombs could be carried out. For a country whose population has recently experienced the loss of six million in a systematic attempt at genocide, these activities will have enormous moral implications.

5. The Holocaust Issue

Israel was brought into being partly as a consequence of the holocaust. In the minds of many, Israel is the antithesis of holocaust. It manifests protection against vulnerability. A Jewish state that is vulnerable to massive, instantaneous destruction will require some getting used to. Such an Israel calls the very premise of the Jewish State into question for many.

6. The Option of War

In a nuclearized Middle East, war is no longer an easy option. It is too dangerous. What will this do to the sense of mastery and active control which Israelis feel over their own destiny? Israel is a society disposed toward action in the face of danger. Everything in Israel's history for the past four decades demonstrates that when in danger, Israel acts. The nuclear situation will bring the country back to the pre-State days of restraint, called the "Havlagah." Transition to restraint despite the capacity to inflict heavy damage on enemies, especially after each terrorist attack, is going to call on new resources in the Israeli public.

7. Territory Is No Longer a Protection

Israelis have been accustomed to regard territory as a protection against infiltration and easy attack. Although Arab countries already have long-range rockets that can hit Israeli cities, their destructive capabilities are not to be compared with atomic weapons. Whatever ability territory has had in the past to protect centers of population becomes redundant in the new atomic reality. Having this or that piece of land loses its importance.

8. The Paradox of Residence

If the enemy includes the effects of fallout in its strategy, the more highly concentrated Jews are among themselves in Israel the more vulnerable they are. The more they are integrated with Arab populations, as in Hebron, the safer they are.

A PROGRAM OF ACTION FOR ISRAELIS

We have presented some of the social psychological issues that a nuclearized Middle East will put on Israel's agenda. Until now a policy of deliberate ambiguity and censorship has prevented public exchanges on these issues. We believe that Israelis must confront the nuclear issue and the devastation it represents. We now offer our outline for a program of action as Israel painfully awakens to the reality of nuclear death.

1. We must not cooperate with those who seek to normalize the issues. Nuclear death is not the death of "the others," it is the death of us all.

2. We must cultivate our awareness that no one can win. Winning is not possible.

3. We must recognize apocalyptic ambitions as insanity, in whichever group they appear, whether Christian, Jewish or Muslim.

4. We must stress that those who rationalize nuclearism rationalize death.

5. We must accept the interests of our species and set them over and above national and religious interests.

6. We must acknowledge that the threat of extinction is greater than the threat from our enemies. We have become brothers with our enemies in our fear of death. We have become vulnerable together.

7. We must recognize that only by actively working for more inclusive identities do we have a chance.

8. We must recognize that the heroism of war is dangerous when it works to glorify war.

9. We must recognize that it is in our own interests for our enemies to develop the same kind of consciousness that we have of this issue.

10. We must accept that there is no way to win in a nuclear age... and no one has the expertise to make decisions for mankind.

Ever since the Holocaust we have proclaimed to ourselves and to the world that we would never allow ourselves to put our head in the sand when faced with a great threat to our existence. In this paper we have examined some of the images of nuclear death and some of the psycho-social issues which prevent us from fulfilling our aim. In an attempt to address these issues, we have suggested some components for an Israeli response to the nuclear threat. Our existence and the continuing existence of humanity is in peril; it is time to take our heads out of the sand.

Bibliography

Avinoam, R. *Deeds of Courage* Vols. 1-12, Israel Defence Ministry, Tel Aviv, 1967 (Hebrew).

———, *Parchments of Fire, An Anthology* Vol. 5, Israel Defence Ministry, Tel Aviv, 1970 (Hebrew).

Berger, P., B. Berger, and H. Kellner, *The Homeless Mind, Modernization and Consciousness*, New York, Vintage Books, 1973.

Blum, A. and P. McHugh. "The Social Ascription of Motives" *American Sociological Review*, Vol. 36 No. 1 (1971) 98-109.

Cassell, E.J. "Being and Becoming Dead" *Social Research*, 29, I:537 Spring (1972).

Cavenar, J.O., J.G. Spaulding, and J.L. Sullivan, "Child's Reaction to Mother's Abortion: Case Report" *Military Medicine*, Vol. 144 (1979) 412-413.

Demske, J. *Being, Man and Death*, Lexington, KY: The University Press of Kentucky, 1970.

Eaton, J. and M. Chen, *Influencing the Youth Culture: A Study of Youth Organizations in Israel*, Beverly Hills, CA, Sage Publishing, 1970.

Elazar, D.J. "The Reconstitution of Jewish Communities in the Post-War Period" *Jewish Journal of Sociology* Vol. XI No. 2 (1969) 187-226.

Golan, A. and A. Shamir, *The Book of Valour* Tel Aviv: Israel Defence Ministry, 1968.

Heidegger, M. *Being and Time* Translated by Macquarrie and Robinson, New York: Harper and Row, 1970.

Kateb, G. "On the Legitimation Crisis" *Social Research* Vol. 46 No. 4, Winter (1979) 695-727.

Krell, R. and L. Rabkin, "The Effects of Sibling Death on the Surviving Child: A Family Perspective" *Family Process* No. 18 (1979) 471-477.

Laqueur, W. *A History of Zionism* London: Weidenfeld and Nicolson, 1972 (p. 561).

Lifton, R.J. "The New Psychology of Human Survival: Images of Doom and Hope" in John Jay College of Criminal Justice, City University of New York, *Center on Violence and Human Survival* Occasional Paper 1, 1986.

Neusner, J. "Now We're All Jews Again" *Response* No. 20 (Winter, 1973), 151-155.

Neusner, J. *Stranger at Home* Chicago: The University of Chicago Press, 1981.

Ney, P.G. "A Consideration of Abortion Survivors" *Child Psychiatry and Human Development* Vol. 13 No. 3 (1982) 166-179.

Pinsker, L. "Auto-Emancipation, 1882" *The Zionist Idea* ed. A. Hertzberg, New York: Harper and Row, 1966.

Ramat Gan, *Fifty-One Medals of Commendation During the War of Attrition* 1968 (Hebrew), *Stories of Those Awarded Medals of Commendation During the War of Attrition,* 1970 (Hebrew).

Rawidowiez, S. *Am-Holech Vamet* Tel Aviv: Metzudah, Vols. 5-6, 1973 (Hebrew).

Roshwald, M. "The Idea of the Promised Land" *Diogenes* No. 82, 45-69.

Shapira, A. *The Seventh Day: Soldier's Talk About the Six-Day War* London: Penguin Books, 1970.

Valery, P. "The Crisis of the Mind" *History and Politics* New York: Pantheon, 1962.

Yehoshua, A.B. Public Address Conference commemorating the death of Lt. David Uzan, Haifa University, Haifa, Israel, May 1972. In Ezer, E.B. *Unease in Zion* New York: Quadrangle, 1974, 395.

Index